INSIDE CHURCHES

A Guide to Church Furnishings
Based on the original edition by Patricia Dirsztay

The National Association
of Decorative & Fine
Arts Societes

© National Association of Decorative and Fine Arts Societies 1993

First edition 1989
Revised edition 1993 by Capability Publishing in association with NADFAS Church Recorders based on the original edition by Patricia Dirsztay.

The National Association of Decorative and Fine Arts Societies, 8a Lower Grosvenor Place, London SW1W 0EN

Capability Publishing Ltd, 10 /11 Lower John Street, London W1R 3PE

Typesetting by Matrix, Down House, Broomhill Road, London SW18 4JQ

Printed by BAS Printers Ltd, Over Wallop, Hampshire

A CIP catalogue record for this book is available from the British Library

ISBN 0 - 9514062 - 2 - 1

Inside Churches has been compiled by the National Association of Decorative and Fine Arts Societies in conjunction with Capability Publishing, who would like to acknowledge with thanks the generous help and advice of the following:

Michael Archer†, Senior Research Assistant (ceramics & glass), Victoria & Albert Museum; David Beasley, Librarian, Goldsmiths' Hall; Jennifer Beazley*; Margaret Bell*; John Blair, The Queens College, Oxford; Chris Blanchett, Tiles & Architectural Ceramics Society; Sheila Chapman*, Pamela Clabburn,textile & embroidery consultant; R.W.M. Clouston; Gerald Cole*, Pamela Cowen, Hon. Secretary, Heritage Co-ordination Group; Barbara Crow*, Patricia Dirsztay; Elizabeth Eames; Donald Findlay, Council for the Care of Churches; Philipa Glanville, Curator, Metalwork Collection, Victoria & Albert Museum; Angela Goedicke*, Chairman, NADFAS Church Recorders; Richard Grasby†; Sarah Greenwood; Richard Hagen†, furniture conservator; Hugh Harrison, Herbert Read Ltd, Ecclesiastical & Domestic Woodcarvers and Joiners; Dr. Mary Hobbs†, Librarian, Chichester Cathedral Library; Dr Doris Jones-Baker; Dr Brian Kemp, Church Monuments Society; Sheelagh Lewis†; Joyce Little*; Nick Norman, retired Master of the Royal Armories; Dr Tony North, Assistant Curator, Metalwork Collection, Victoria & Albert Museum; Ian Pickford†; Dr John Richardson, Secretary, The Pewter Society; Tom Robinson, Chairman, The Antiquarian Horological Society; the Revd Richard Robson, Curator, The Castle Howard Costume Galleries; Madeau Stewart; Elliott Viney, Trustee, Patricia Fay Memorial Fund; Lt Col JF Willcocks†, NADFAS Heraldry Adviser; Dr Donald Wright, British Institute of Organ Studies; Doreen Yarwood†.

Drawings: (first edition) Caroline Cook, Frances Curwen and Paul Vincent.
Additional Drawings: (second edition) Paul Vincent and Doreen Yarwood.

* members of NADFAS Church Recorders
† NADFAS lecturer

PREFACE

*The Most Reverend George Carey,
Archbishop of Canterbury*

It is one of the privileges of my ministry to worship in many beautiful cathedrals and parish churches. They are almost always cared for lovingly. But I am conscious that we should not take our inheritance of historic buildings for granted. As social needs change and our communities become more mobile, parish churches become more vulnerable. Most communities know more or less what their church looks like, but even the most committed members of the parish may be surprisingly unaware of the significance of the decoration and the furniture which their church contains. It is not just that churches are places of peace and beauty, but also that they have so much to tell us of our own history.

This book will help all of us to interpret that history. Its publication celebrates the work of the Church Recorders of the National Association of Decorative and Fine Arts Societies and marks their Twentieth Anniversary. For twenty years, small groups of amateur enthusiasts have been painstakingly recording every item of furniture and interior decoration in parish churches, large and small, all over the country. Their efforts form the only national inventory of the contents of our hundreds of churches today. The importance of this Record for the future conservation and preservation of churches cannot be overestimated; without it we should have very little idea of where to start.

I congratulate the Church Recorders on twenty valuable years' dedication to the conservation of our churches. Perhaps we should also congratulate them for sharing their knowledge in making this book available, so that we all have an opportunity to understand and enjoy what we see around us in our churches.

CONTENTS

CONTENTS

CONTENTS

AN INTRODUCTION TO THE HISTORY OF THE CHURCH IN BRITAIN

Churches in Britain encapsulate much of the complex history of these islands. Nearly every town and village has its own parish church and most often it is the oldest building, set apart from the dwellings of ordinary people. Many churches are truly ancient, the first buildings in stone by early Christians, dating back to a time when religion was the main spring of society. It is not uncommon to find a church built by the Norman settlers of the 11th century but it is unusual for any church to date from only one century; many have something to offer from every period of our history. From the start, the shape, decoration and furnishings of our cathedrals and parish churches have been governed by the services held in them.

Although there has been a constant evolution over the centuries, we can recognise three distinct periods: the six hundred years to the Reformation in the mid-16th century; the next three hundred years during which a whole series of fundamental changes were followed by a period of stagnation; and finally a re-awakening from the 1840's to today.

The Medieval Centuries

The entire medieval period was dominated by its religion and, in protestant times, it is easy to forget that medieval religion was an international one, based on a complex ritual centred on the Pope in Rome. Early churches were, therefore, Roman Catholic.

The Anglo-Saxons can have had few furnishings in their places of worship, apart from the cup used at Mass. From the earliest times, there would have been a font for baptism and, because it is usually free-standing, the font has often survived from Norman times even if the church around it has been entirely rebuilt. The Normans built many small stone 3 or 4 cell churches with a small chancel and a slightly larger nave. In the earliest, processions around a tomb of a saint or bishop were an essential part of ritual and a rounded apse at the east end of the church provided space. As churches increased in size, the aisles took over this function and the east end tended to be flattened.

The 11th and 12th centuries were the great period of monasticism. Many churches were bequeathed by their lay patrons to a wealthy cathedral or abbey. From earliest times, the chancel had been the responsibility of the priest and the nave of the parish. With the appointment of church wardens from 1129, the laiety had more influence on changes in the main body of the church. The patronage of wealthy benefactors encouraged a proliferation of new aisles, steeples, porches, towers and clerestory windows all of which fundamentally affected the appearance of the church.

The 12th and 15th centuries saw a period of extraordinary decorative innovation. Perhaps the most significant was the arrival of stained glass, in cathedrals from the 1170's and in parish churches in the 13th century. At the same time wall paintings began to appear, covering the nave walls with biblical scenes and always focused on the great Doom or Day of Judgement over the chancel and above the rood. In the 13th century mass would have been said daily. A traveller entering the south door would have first seen the figure of St Christopher painted on the opposite wall. The single Sanctus bell would have told him that the service was starting; it would have rung again at the Elevation of the Host. Mass could only be said once daily at any particular altar, so as the number of priests grew, it became necessary to have additional altars, often placed at the east end of the side-aisles, so that separate chapels within the main body of the church were formed.

Not many medieval churches had pulpits. Preaching was more often done by friars at the village cross which could be in the churchyard or on the village green. In the 13th century, fonts were covered to protect the consecrated water from theft. It seems that the consecrated water was seldom changed.

Memorials began to appear. For centuries they were confined to the graves of priests and great men. At first, even the grandest had only a simple cross incised on their tomb slabs. These developed into figures of recumbent knights and ladies, first in stone and then in alabaster. The less ambitious or those who could not afford a massive stone or marble monument were content with a decorated brass memorial. The earliest brass in England is dated 1277 and they continued to be popular until the early 17th century.

The Black Death, or bubonic plague, that swept the country in the mid-14th century was a social and economic disaster but it had another long term effect in encouraging a general acceptance of the uncertainty of life and an increasing concern for the after-life. The wealthy began to build chantry chapels, endowing them with a priest to pray perpetually for their souls. The obsession with death can be seen in the skulls and skeletons carved into monuments.

In the century before the Reformation, there was much rebuilding, particularly in the counties which prospered from the wool trade, but everywhere towers were being added to the west end of churches. These were principally to house a set of bells, but there was undoubtedly rivalry between neighbouring parishes to build the grandest or the highest tower. Two other developments mark the 15th century. The introduction of simple benches for seating and the substitution of the old steep pitched roof by a flatter one which made possible the insertion of a new tier of clerestory windows high above the nave.

The Anglican Church

The immediate effect of the Reformation in the 1530's was devastating. The new religion was based on preaching and the community and its churches were plain and unadorned; the colourful arenas of the medieval saints were no longer acceptable.

An obsession with idolatry meant the destruction of almost all visible decoration. Wall paintings were whitewashed, fonts and monuments defaced, stone altars and the rood removed, plate and vestments confiscated and much stained glass destroyed. For the first time, laymen could enter the chancel whether the dividing rood screen had been destroyed or not. A new wooden Holy Table took the place of the stone altar.

To accommodate the changed needs of the changed liturgy, in the 17th century, a number of new furnishings appeared. The new Anglican service emphasised Mattins and Evensong so the Eucharist or communion mass became an occasional service. Since preaching was the most important element of these services, for the next two hundred years the pulpit was the dominant feature in most churches. Pulpits were set high because they had to place the preacher above the new box pews and the tester above helped to carry the preacher's words to the ends of the church.

Other innovations of these years were the Poorbox and the Breadbasket for the distribution of alms to the poor, based on the medieval monastic system of Bread Dole. The display of The Sentences (Lord's Prayer, Creed and Ten Commandments), made obligatory in churches in 1603, and the Royal Arms, signifying the monarch as Head of the Church, became a universal ornament after 1662. In the 1630's, Archbishop Laud introduced altar rails to prevent dogs from approaching the Table.

Almost no new churches were built between the Reformation and the Great Fire of London after which a radically different style of church design appeared, classical in form and planned to accommodate the contemporary liturgy. Architects like Wren, Hawksmoor and Gibbs saw churches as preaching boxes, rectangular halls with galleries, plain glass in round-headed windows, no east window but a reredos behind the altar, probably incorporating the Sentences, box pews and a dominating pulpit. Magnificent new plate was donated by patrons and, in country churches, hatchments were set high on the walls when the local squire died. This was the great age of English sculpture and magnificent, but often overlarge, monuments filled the chancel.

The Victorian Revival and After

The Church of England dozed through the late 18th and early 19th centuries, leaving churches generally damp, decaying and uncared for until the electric impact of the Oxford Movement in the 1840's jerked the Church out of its inertia. With the Ecclesiologists in command, there began a revolution which, in 30 years, restored or built the majority of parish churches, saving many from total decay but destroying or distorting much of beauty and antiquity in the process. A reaction against the Carolean and Georgian periods meant the loss of box pews and many pulpits and the removal of classical monuments to more obscure parts of the building. The musicians in the west gallery were replaced by a surpliced choir in the chancel backed by an organ. There were new brass lecterns, altarcloths, vestments, new tiles on the floor and new stained glass (of very varying quality) in the windows. Pulpits were rebuilt in stone and fonts, which had become much smaller after the Reformation when total immersion at baptism ceased, returned to their medieval size.

There have been changes enough since then. Today's churches offer us a mix and amalgam of all periods and architectural styles. Search for it and there is evidence to be found of every period of the church's gradual evolution. Radical changes in belief and liturgy produced sudden new directions. We can trace them through the objects, decoration and furnishings they left behind. It is the sheer variety of Britain's churches and the historical breadth that they incorporate that combines to ensure their perennial fascination.

How to Use This Guide

Inside Churches is a practical reference book. It will help you to name and identify the furnishings of any parish church or cathedral in Britain. This is how it works....

At the front is a **general introduction** to the history of the church in Britain from earliest times until today. The book is organised in three overall sections:

Styles and Terminology chapters will tell you HOW to describe the things you see

Materials chapters will tell you WHAT you see depending whether it is made of wood, metal, paper, cloth or stone.

Objects chapters will tell you WHAT it is if it falls into one of several special categories; clocks; memorials and monuments; musical instruments; windows.

Sections are divided into chapters and chapters into sub-sections dealing with specific groups of styles or objects.

If, for example, you are looking at a piece of furniture. Is it made of wood? Turn to the MATERIALS section then to the WOOD chapter. At the beginning of the chapter you find a glossary of the special terms used to describe types of wood and types of decoration and construction specific to this material. If your piece of furniture looks like a table, turn to the sub-section TABLES. Does it look like any of the illustrated examples? If so, you will find either its name and, perhaps, date or even a full description of it using the correct terms. If you can find no similar illustration, turn back to the front of the chapter to identify its constituent parts (legs, feet and backs give the most clues). Turn to the STYLES AND TERMINOLOGY section for information on the decoration and date.

Using the book, you will have found out exactly what it is, what it was used for, approximately how old it might be and how to describe it. If you already know what the object is but want to learn more, or if you come across a term that is unfamiliar, turn to the **Index** in the back of the book.

Throughout the text, proper names are in highlighted thus   Credence:
descriptions are in roman type, thus   of trestle form;
and explanations are in brackets in italic type, thus   *(sanctuary table).*

Inside Churches' primary aim is to help people record the objects and decoration in churches. CHURCH RECORDERS will find notes in italics at the foot of those sections where particular recording techniques are advised. In general, however, you will need to describe the object in detail noting decoration, colour, position, inscriptions or maker's name and its state of preservation. Add photographs and sketch drawings where you can.

If you want more information on Church Recorders, write to:
Church Recorders, The National Association of Decorative and Fine Arts Societies, 8a Lower Grosvenor Place, London SW1W 0EN.

Inside Churches will give you an introduction to a wide number of decorative and fine arts and help increase your knowledge of church interiors. However, it would not be practical to answer all your questions, so if you want to know more about any particular aspect, turn to FURTHER READING for a selection of reference books.

STYLES & TERMINOLOGY

ARCHITECTURE
Terms

The main decorative periods of British Church Art and Architecture are:

650-1050	Saxon
1050-1200	Romanesque (Norman)
1175-1550	**GOTHIC:**
1175-1300	Early English
1300-1380	Decorated
1380-1550	Perpendicular
1550-1600	Elizabethan
1600-1650	Early Stuart
1650-1670	Artisan Mannerist
1670-1690	Restoration
1690-1720	Baroque
1720-1830	**GEORGIAN:**
1720-1760	Palladian
1760-1790	Neoclassical
1790-1830	Regency
1830-1890	Victorian
1890-1920	Arts and Crafts
	Art Nouveau
1920-1940	Art Deco
	Thirties
1950-1965	Modernist
1965-1980	Brutalist
1980-	Post-Modern

THE CHURCH
Christian churches are most often cruiform in shape with the altar at the eastern end.

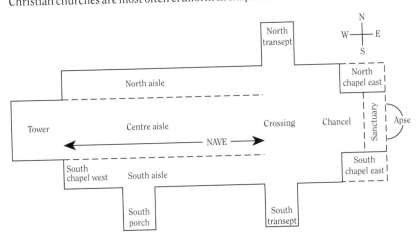

ABACUS
The slab on top of a **capital** on which the **architrave** rests;
the shape varies according to the **Order**.

Lugged or eared architrave

ARCHITRAVE
The moulded frame surrounding a door or window. It is also the lowest main division of the **entablature**, between the **frieze** and **abacus**. A **lintel** is the horizontal member over a door or window.

CORNICE
The uppermost member of a entablature, surmounting the frieze, or any moulded projection which crowns the part to which it is fixed, eg. wall, door, column, piece of furniture, window, panelling, etc.

FRIEZE
A decorative band between the architrave and cornice or, in furniture, between the cornice and framework.

IMPOST
The slab, usually moulded, on which the ends of an arch rest.

PEDIMENT
An ornamental low pitched triangular or segmental gable above the cornice of an entablature.

Triangular

Segmental

Swan-necked

Broken

Open

Scrolled

Spur

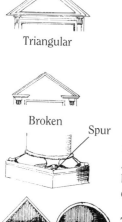

SPUR
An ornamental protrusion on the corner between the base of a **column** or **pillar** and the **plinth**. Also a fixed draught **screen**, or a **buttress**.

TYMPANUM
The filled-in space of a pediment or of the curved section of an arch.

ARCHITECTURE
Terms

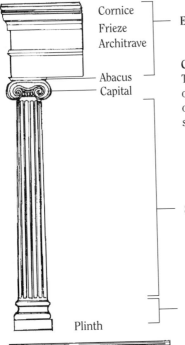

Cornice
Frieze ⎱ — Entablature
Architrave

Abacus
Capital

COLUMNS
The horizontal members above a column resting on the abacus *(which is part of the capital)*. Parts of an entablature may also be on a wall or other structure without columnar support

— Shaft

— Base

Plinth

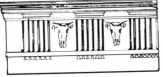

Doric frieze with **mutules** *(projecting brackets)* above **triglyphs** *(grooved tablets)* alternating with **metopes** *(square spaces)* here containing bucrania and with **guttae** *(drops)* below

Ionic Capital   with angle volutes

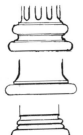

BASES
Attic Base   **scotia** *(concave moulding)* between two
tori *(large convex mouldings)*

Tuscan Base   torus with a fillet above

Base   with two **astragals** *(small convex moulding)* with a scotia above and a torus below

4

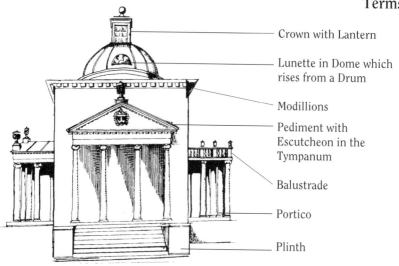

Crown with Lantern

Lunette in Dome which rises from a Drum

Modillions

Pediment with Escutcheon in the Tympanum

Balustrade

Portico

Plinth

ARCADE
A series of arches supported on piers or columns.

Hatchment in Spandrel

Respond *(a half pillar or shaft engaged with a wall to support an arch, usually at the end of an arcade).*

Dado rail returned, continuing at right angles along the end wall.

Acroterion	ornament at apex or lower angles of pediment
Stylobate	continuous base supporting a colonnade

The term **column** in classical architecture is an upright structural member of round or polygonal section with a shaft, a capital and usually, a base. The term **pillar** is used in Gothic architecture (see p. 6).

DORIC is distinguished by triglyphs and metopes in the frieze and mutules under the corona.
Greek Doric has a fluted shaft and no base.
Roman Doric has an attic base and fluted or plain shaft.

IONIC has volutes on the capital and dentils in the cornice, a fluted shaft and an attic base.

CORINTHIAN has a fluted shaft, a capital ornamented with acanthus, olive or laurel leaves, eight small volutes and an attic base.

TUSCAN is simplified Doric

COMPOSITE is an ornate version of Corinthian and occurs in various forms

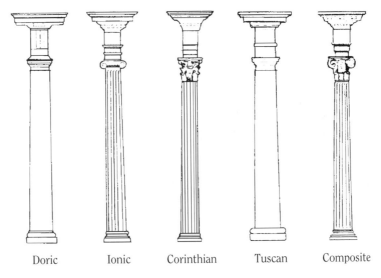

Doric   Ionic   Corinthian   Tuscan   Composite

OTHER CAPITALS

 Cushion
Norman

Scalloped
Norman

Waterleaf
12th century

Crocket
Transitional

 Stiff Leaf
13th century

 Natural Leaf
14th century

 Engaged Column

 Pilaster Strip
(thin pilaster without base or capital)

 Colonnettes
(diminutive columns)

 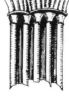 Compound Pier

 Pillar
(solid detached upright support in Gothic architecture)

Blind Arcade

 Pillar of clustered shafts
(often misnamed as clustered column)

 Pilaster
(rectangular support projecting slightly from a surface, with base and capital)

Colonnade

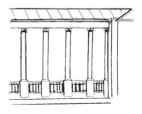

ARCHITECTURE
Arches

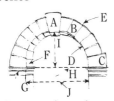

1. Structure of an arch

A Keystone	F Soffit
B Voussoir	G Impost
C Springer	H Springing Line
D Intrados	I Rise
E Extrados	J Span

An **arch** is a structure of wedge-shaped blocks of stone, brick or concrete covering an opening which support one another by mutual pressure and are thus capable of carrying considerable weight (1).

The Etruscans constructed arches composed of radiating blocks (**voussoirs**); a number of examples survive in town gateways of central Italy as at Volterra. The Romans then adapted this method of construction extensively in order to suit their more complex needs (2).

The classical arch, whether ancient Roman, Renaissance or Modern is, therefore, round-headed as is also the Romanesque (Norman) design which, as the name suggests, is derived from Rome (3, 4).

The most important feature of Gothic architecture, introduced in the late 12th century, was the pointed arch or, as the French aptly term it, the **arc brisé**. The early form was narrow and sharply pointed, the **lancet** or Early English shape (6).

2. Arch of Titus, Rome AD 81

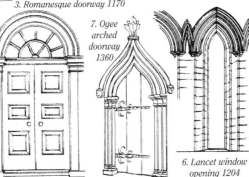

3. Romanesque doorway 1170

8. Four-centred arched gateway 1510

5. Gothic doorway (equilateral arch) c. 1300

7. Ogee arched doorway 1360

4. Classical doorway 1713-14

6. Lancet window opening 1204

Gradually the arch widened to the equilateral form where height was equal to width. Later variations included, for example, the ogee with its double curve form, concave to convex (7) and the late medieval four-centred shape of two different convex curves (8).

Drawings by Doreen Yarwood *Chronology of Western Architecture*, Batsford

AEDICULE

A classical architectural surround to an opening *(door, window, niche, etc)* composed of columns and an entablature, sometimes with a pediment.

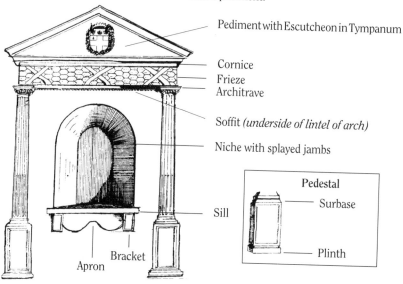

Pediment with Escutcheon in Tympanum

Cornice
Frieze
Architrave

Soffit *(underside of lintel of arch)*

Niche with splayed jambs

Pedestal
Surbase

Sill

Plinth

Bracket
Apron

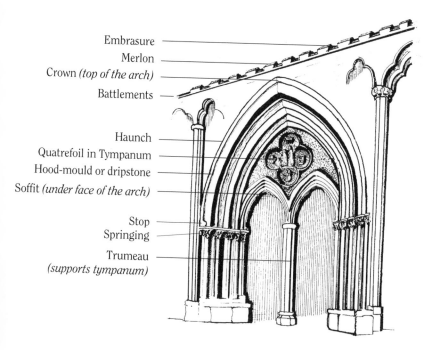

Embrasure
Merlon
Crown *(top of the arch)*
Battlements

Haunch
Quatrefoil in Tympanum
Hood-mould or dripstone
Soffit *(under face of the arch)*

Stop
Springing
Trumeau
(supports tympanum)

9

ARCHITECTURE
Timber Trussed Roofs

Such open roofs, constructed of massive timbers, were developed from the early Middle Ages and covered many church roof interiors until the early 20th century. The word **truss** is given to the system of timbers, each of which was tenoned and pinned to provide a stable structure which would resist all thrusts.

In general, the medieval roof was gabled at each end with a fairly steep pitch. A long beam, the **ridge pole** or **piece**, extended horizontally along the apex from one end of the roof to the other. Further beams, the **purlins**, were set at intervals parallel to the ridge pole and at the top edge of the walls were placed very heavy beams called **wall plates**, secured by stone **corbels**. At right angles to these timbers were fixed the rafters which extended from wall plate to ridge. The simplest truss was developed early in the Middle Ages. This was the tie beam structure. In this a massive beam was thrown across the nave or choir at wall plate level to counteract the outward thrust of the roof upon the walls. On this tie beam was generally set a central vertical post rising from tie beam to ridge pole, a **king post**. Sometimes a pair of such posts were used, **queen posts**. Alternatively a **crown post** was used, in this case a vertical post extended from the centre of the tie beam to a higher horizontal beam, the **collar beam**. In all cases straight struts and curved braces were introduced as reinforcement was needed.

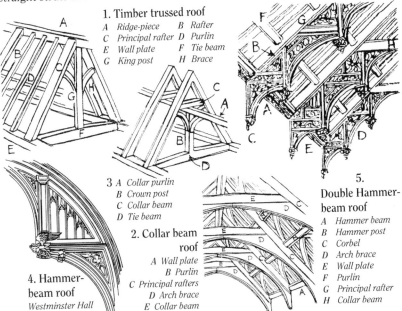

1. Timber trussed roof
A Ridge-piece B Rafter
C Principal rafter D Purlin
E Wall plate F Tie beam
G King post H Brace

3 A Collar purlin
B Crown post
C Collar beam
D Tie beam

2. Collar beam roof
A Wall plate
B Purlin
C Principal rafters
D Arch brace
E Collar beam

4. Hammer-beam roof
Westminster Hall

5.
Double Hammer-beam roof
A Hammer beam
B Hammer post
C Corbel
D Arch brace
E Wall plate
F Purlin
G Principal rafter
H Collar beam

Drawings by Doreen Yarwood. *English Interiors* Lutterworth Press.

A later, more complex, phase could be seen in the **hammerbeam** roof design which was developed in the late 14th century. Hammerbeams resembled cut-off tie beams. They extended at wall plate level and were supported from corbels by means of arch-braced wall posts: both corbels and hammerbeam ends were generally decoratively carved. The shorter hammerbeams gave better visibility than the tie beams and reduced lateral pressure. Vertical hammer posts rose from the inner end of the hammerbeams to a collar beam above.

The sanctuary is the focal point of the church. Although its arrangement is not strictly architectural much architectural terminology is used to describe it. The arrangement will differ according to the form of the service. In Anglican churches, the Sacrament will generally be kept in an **aumbry** or **hanging pyx**. In Roman Catholic churches, the Sacrament is generally kept in a **tabernacle** on the altar.

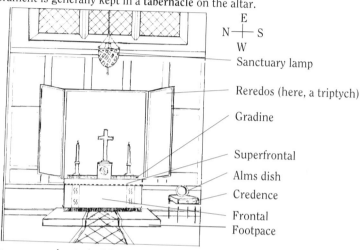

E
N ─┼─ S
W

— Sanctuary lamp

— Reredos (here, a triptych)

— Gradine

— Superfrontal

— Alms dish

— Credence

— Frontal

— Footpace

Altar	elevated slab or wooden table used for the celebration of Holy Communion.
Antependium	movable panel of carved or painted wood or metal serving as a front cover for the altar
Aumbry	two accepted uses: first, a recessed cupboard in the wall of a church (anywhere in the building, for any use) and secondly the specific use of such a cupboard, normally on the north side of the high altar or Lady Chapel altar, as a place in which the Blessed Sacrament is reserved.
Credence	table or shelf on south side of the altar used for the sacramental elements and vessels during Communion Services.
Footpace	step on which the altar stands, returning to the East wall rather than running across the sanctuary.
Frontal	textile forming covering for the front of an altar.
Gradine	shelf at rear of the altar top, sometimes attached to the Reredos.
Laudian pall	loose 3 or 4-sided throw-over altar covering reaching to the gound on all sides.
Predella	a subsidary panel or series of panels, below the main representation in an altarpiece or a stained glass window.
Reredos	fixed screen behind and above the altar: **Altarpiece**, if it is a painting; **Dossal**, if it is a curtain; **Diptych** (2 panels) or **Triptych** (3 panels), if a hinged painting or panel.
Superfrontal	band of material, usually fringed and sometimes contrasting, overlapping the upper edge of the frontal.
Tabernacle	receptable for the Reserved Sacrament. A box-like structure placed in the centre of the altar and generally used in Roman Catholic churches.

ATTRIBUTES AND ALLEGORY
Saints

Biblical stories depicted in stained glass, sculpture and painted scenes had to be understood by people who could not read. Through the medieval period a complex iconography developed linking every saint, apostle or biblical personality with an image which identified him with the event that gave him prominence. Today, these images are often incomprehensible because we no longer understand the references.

SAINTS' ATTRIBUTES
Images of Saints were easily identified by medieval people by the symbols or attributes they carried. A woman holding a wheel, for example, is probably Catherine of Alexandria who was martyred on a wheel.

Saints usually have more than one attribute and the combination of several helps to identify them. A dragon, for example, is associated with several saints, but one next to, or below, a winged figure (often in armour) identifies St Michael, whereas one associated with a knight without wings will identify St George. Attributes are not depicted consistently in the same way, eg. St Ursula sometimes holds an arrow and is sometimes pierced by one.

Saints are listed first by attribute and then by name. Their accustomed dress is not strictly an attribute, but is included as one where appropriate since it may be an important identifying characteristic.

BEASTS AND MEN

Attribute	Saint
Cow	Bridgit of Kildare
Does (2)	Withburga
Dog	Roch, with plague sore on leg
Dogs (2)	Dominic, with black and white dogs holding torches in mouths
Dragon & cross	Margaret of Antioch
Dragon	Archangel Michael (winged); George, usually in armour;
Dragon led by chain	Juliana of Nicanedia
Dragon led by rope or ribbon	Martha
Horse, white	George
Lamb	Agnes; Francis of Assisi; John the Baptist
Lion & raven	Vincent of Sarogossa
Lion (winged)	Mark
Lion	Euphemia or Jerome
Man (winged)	Matthew
Mule (kneeling)	Anthony of Padua
Otter	Bishop Cuthbert
Ox (winged)	Luke
Oxen (2)	Walstan, who also holds scythe
Pig, boar or hog	Anthony of Egypt (Anthony Abbot)
Sheep	Genevieve
Stag (crucifix between horns)	Eustace or Hubert
Wolf (guarding head)	Edmund
Wolf, Lion or Cock	Vitus

BIRDS

Attribute	Saint
Birds	Francis of Assisi
Cock	Peter
Cock, lion or wolf	Vitus
Dove on sceptre	King Edmund
Dove on shoulder	David of Wales
Dove	Pope Gregory
Doves in cage or basket (2)	Joseph or Joachim
Eagle	John the Evangelist
Swan & flowers	Hugh of Lincoln

OBJECTS AND FLOWERS

Anchor	Clement or Nicholas of Myra
Anvil	Adrian or Bishop Eloi
Armour (winged with dragon)	Michael
Armour (no wings and with dragon)	George
Arrow (in hand)	Ursula
Arrow (piercing breast or hand)	Giles
Arrow	Edmund
Arrows (pierced by and bound to tree or column)	Sebastian (naked)
Axe	Matthias
Axe (in head)	Peter the Martyr
Bag of money	Matthew or Judas Iscariot
Balls (3)	Nicholas of Myra
Banner (red cross & surrounded by virgins)	Ursula
Basket of fruit & flowers	Dorothea/Dorothy
Basket or pitcher	Zita
Basket with loaves	Philip
Beehive	Ambrose; Bernard of Clairvaux; John Chrysostom
Beggar	Edith of Wilton (washing feet of beggar)
Beggar (receiving cloak)	Martin
Bell	Anthony Abbot
Bones	Ambrose
Book	many saints hold a gospel
Book	Virgin Mary in Annunciation & as Mary, Mother of all Wisdom
Book & crook	Chad
Books	Ambrose or Boniface
Bottle/pilgrim flask	James the Great
Box or vase	Mary Magdalene (with long hair)
Breasts, on plate	Agatha
Candle (devil blowing it out)	Genevieve

Capstan	Erasmus, Bishop of Formiae or Elmo
Cauldron of oil	Vitus
Chains	Leonard or Peter (in prison)
Child on arm	Anthony of Padua
Child Jesus on shoulder	Christopher (crossing river)
Child, crucified	William of Norwich
Children (male) carried (2)	Eustace
Children in tub (3)	Nicholas of Myra
Children, male (2)	Mary, wife of Cleophas
Church (model of)	Withburga (2 does at feet) or Botolph or other founder
Cloth (imprinted with face of Christ)	Veronica
Comb (iron)	Bishop Blaise
Cross (inverted)	Peter
Cross (red on white)	George
Cross (saltire)	Andrew
Crown of roses	Cecilia
Crown of roses or holding roses	Dorothy or Teresa
Demon at feet	Norbert (in white habit)
Devil trampled on by man in armour	Michael
Devil with bellows	Genevieve
Drug jars	Cosmas and Damian
Eyes on dish	Lucy
Flame in hand/breast	Anthony of Padua
Fuller's club	James the Less
Gridiron	Laurence or Vincent
Halberd	Jude
Head (own, carried before altar)	Winefride or Osyth
Head (own, crowned & carried)	Bishop Cuthbert or Bishop Denis
Head (man's under feet)	Catherine of Alexandria
Heart (flaming or transfixed by sword)	Augustine of Hippo

ATTRIBUTES AND ALLEGORY
Saints

Attribute	Saint
Hermit	Anthony Abbot
Horseshoe	Bishop Eloi
Idols (broken)	Wilfrid (baptising pagans)
Keys	Peter; Zita; Martha (at girdle)
Knife & skin over arm	Bartholomew
Lily	Euphemia; Joseph; Dominic (in black & white habit); Catherine of Siena (usually in Dominican habit)
Loaves	Olaf & Zita
Loaves & fishes	disciples
Manacles	Leonard (holding them)
Medical equipment	Cosmas & Damian
Millstone	Vincent
Musical instruments	Cecilia
Olive branch	Agnes
Pagans being baptised	Wilfrid
Palm leaf	any martyr
Peacock feather	Barbara
Pen, ink & scroll	Mark; Matthew; Bernard of Clairvaux
Pincers	Agatha; Dunstan; Apollonia (holding tooth)
Portrait of Virgin Mary	Luke
Roses in lap	Elizabeth of Hungary
Pot of holy water & aspergillum	Martha (or as housewife, with kitchen pot & ladle)
Saw	Simon
Scallop shell	James the Great
Scourge	Ambrose
Scythe & carrying head	Sidwell or Sithewell
Scythe & oxen (2)	Walstan
Set-square	Thomas
Shears	Agatha
Sieve (broken)	Benedict
Staff	James the Great; James the Less; Bridget of Sweden or Anthony Abbot
Stone (striking head)	Stephen
Sword	Paul or Barbara
Sword through breast	Euphemia
Sword through neck	Lucy
T-shaped or Tau cross	Philip
T-shaped or Tau cross on shoulder	Anthony Abbot
Together	Cosmas & Damian; Raphael & Tobias; (carrying fish); Peter & Paul; Philip & James
Tower	Barbara
Tree	Etheldreda (asleep)
Tree (foot on fallen tree)	Bishop Boniface
True Cross	Helen
Weighing souls	Michael
Wheel	Catherine of Alexandria (man's head under feet)
Winged man	Matthew
Wounded forehead (red band)	Bridget of Sweden
Wounded leg	Roch (also with angel, dog, staff or shell)
Wounds of Christ (stigmata)	Francis of Assisi

SAINTS AND APOSTLES

Apostles are marked ★, there are always 12, but not always the same saints. Jude, Simon and Matthias are not always included. Apostles may also carry scrolls which contain the creed. The principal attribute of each saint is highlighted and shown first.

Adrian	**anvil**; axe; sword
Agatha	**dish containing her breasts**; pincers; shears
Agnes	**lamb**; olive branch; palm
Aidan	**flaming torch**; stag at feet;
Alban	**sword**; fountain; his head in his hands; mace
Alphege	**chasuble full of stones**
Ambrose	**beehive**; books; 2 human bones; scourge with 3 knots
★ Andrew	**saltire cross**
Anthony Abbot	**stick with T-shaped handle** or Tau cross on shoulder; bell; pig; fire
Anthony of Padua	**Franciscan habit**; infant Christ in arms; flame in hand or on breast; kneeling mules
Apollonia	**pincers holding tooth**
Augustine of Canterbury	**dressed as archbishop**
Augustine of Hippo	**flaming heart transfixed by 2 arrows**; dressed as bishop; books
Barbara	**tower**; cup and wafer; peacock's feather; cannon; crown
★ Barnabas	**Tudor roses** on shield or gospel
★ Bartholomew	**knife**; his skin held over his arm
Benedict	**Benedictine habit** (black, or white of the reformed order); broken cup; sprinkler; raven with loaf in beak; broken sieve
Bernard of Clairvaux	**white habit with pastoral staff**; beehive; inkhorn; pen; 3 mitres; bound dragon
Blaise	**iron comb**; dressed as bishop
Boniface	**book transfixed by sword** or stained with blood; foot on fallen tree; dressed as archbishop
Botolph	**dressed as abbot**
Bridget of Sweden	**taper or candle**; crozier; staff; red band across forehead
Catherine of Alexandria	**wheel**; head of man under feet; sword and book
Catherine of Siena	**cross with lily**; white tunic and veil with black cloak; book or rosary in hands
Cecilia	**musical instruments**; crown of roses
Chad	**St. Chad's cross**; book and crook
Christopher	**carrying infant Christ across river**
Clare	**pyx or monstrance**; dressed as nun; cross; lily
Clement	**anchor**; dressed as Pope or bishop
Cosmas & Damian	**medical equipment**; always together; dressed as physicians
Cuthbert	**St Oswald's crowned head in hands**; dressed as bishop; otter
David of Wales	**dove on shoulder**; dressed as bishop; bible
Denis	**dressed as bishop; carries his own head**
Dominic	**black and white dogs with torch in mouth**; star on forehead; lily; black and white habit
Dorothea/Dorothy	**basket of roses**; roses and apples; crown of roses
Dunstan	**gold cup on blue field**; red hot pincers

ATTRIBUTES & ALLEGORY
Saints

Edith of Wilton	washing feet of beggar
Edmund	crowned and pierced by arrows; dressed as king; wolf guarding head; arrow
Edward	dressed as king; sceptre surmounted by dove; ring
Elizabeth	in Salutation scenes and with her son, John the Baptist
Eloi or Eligius	anvil; dressed as bishop; hammer and tongs; horseshoe; bellows at feet
Erasmus	capstan; dressed as bishop; sailing ship
Etheldreda	dressed as nun; crowned; building church; asleep under tree
Euphemia	sword through breast; lion; bear; lily
Eustace	stag with crucifix between horns; carrying his 2 sons across river; brass bull
Francis of Assisi	birds; lamb; lily; stigmata
Frideswide	dressed as abbess, crowned; gospels
Genevieve	crook or distaff; dressed as nun; devil blowing out lighted candle relit by angel; sheep; basket of loaves
George	red cross on white ground on banner or breast; white horse; dragon
Giles	hind pierced by arrow; arrow piercing hand and stag
Gregory	dressed as pope; dove on shoulder; dove hovering overhead
Helena	dressed as empress; large cross (True cross)
Hubert	dressed as hunter or bishop; stag with crucifix between horns, beside him or crouched on book
Hugh of Lincoln	swan; Carthusian habit; 3 flowers
Ives or Yvo	dressed as lawyer; surrounded by widows and orphans
★ James the Great	scallop shell; staff; bottle; pilgrim's broad-brimmed hat
★ James the Less	fuller's staff or club
Jerome	cardinal's hat; lion; as man of learning at desk or in desert
Joachim	meeting St Anne at Golden Gate; basket with 2 doves
John Chrysostom	dove at ear; beehive; chalice; gospels
John de Matha	white habit with blue/red cross on breast; fetters; angels leading captives
John the Baptist	hairy coat; lamb; tall staff with cross piece;
★ John the Evangelist	eagle; cup with serpent
Joseph	flowering rod; doves in cage or basket
Joseph of Arimathaea	shroud; crown of thorns; nails
★ Jude	halberd; club; lance
Julian of le Mans	blue cross-crosslet saltire wise, on silver shield
Juliana of Nicanedia	devil flogged or held in chains
Laurence	gridiron
Leonard	broken fetters; dressed as deacon or abbot; holding chains; manacles
Louis IX	crown of thorns; dressed as king or Franciscan; 3 nails of the cross
Lucy	eyes in dish; lamp; sword; wound in neck
★ Luke the Evangelist	winged ox; painting a portrait of Virgin Mary
Margaret of Antioch	rising from belly of dragon; dragon; palm; cross

ATTRIBUTES & ALLEGORY

Saint	Attributes
★ Mark the Evangelist	winged lion; pen; ink; scroll
Martha	leading dragon; aspergillum; ladle; keys at girdle;
Martin	giving half cloak to beggar; dressed as bishop; goose at feet
Mary, dau. of Cleophas	4 sons (James the Less, Jude, Simon, Joseph) & their attributes
Mary, dau. of Salomar	2 sons (John the Evangelist, James the Great) & their attributes
Mary Magdalene	vase or box of ointment; long blonde hair; or as Penitant Harlot, barely clothed usually holding a crucifix and with a skull beside her, sometimes her cast-off jewellery at her feet
★ Matthew the Evangelist	winged man; ink; scroll; pen; bag of money; knife; dagger
★ Matthias	axe; halberd
Nicholas of Myra	3 golden balls or purses; dressed as bishop; ship; anchor; 3 children in tub
Norbert	dressed in white habit over black; devil bound at feet; spider in chalice; monstrance or ciborium
Olaf	loaves
Oswald	dressed as king; sceptre; cross; silver dish
Osyth or Sytha	dressed as queen or abbess; own head in hands
★ Paul	sword; beard
★ Peter	keys; fish; inverted cross; beard; curly hair
Peter the Martyr	dressed as Dominican; wound in head
★ Philip	cross; T-shaped cross; basket of loaves
Radegunda	dressed as abbess (crowned); kneeling captive at feet; holding broken fetters
Roch	pointing at plague sore on leg; dog; staff; shell; angel
Sebastian	bound to tree or column; pierced by arrows
Sidwell or Sithewell	scythe; well; head in hands
★ Simon	saw; fishes; cross
Stephen	stone striking head ; dressed as deacon
Swithin	dressed as bishop (Winchester)
Sylvester	bound; dressed as pope; 2 dead pagans; spear; dagger
Teresa of Avila	dressed in brown habit; roses; dragon
★ Thomas	builder's set-square; ruler; girdle
Thomas à Becket	dressed as archbishop or Benedictine; wound in head
Thomas Aquinas	dressed as Dominican; star on breast
Ursula	arrow in hand or pierced by one; surrounded by handmaidens; banner (red cross on white)
Veronica	cloth marked with head of Christ
Vincent	dressed as deacon; raven; gridiron; millstone; whip in hand
Vitus	cauldron of oil; boy with palm; cock; lion; wolf
Walstan	crowned; scythe in hand; 2 oxen at feet
Wilfrid	baptising pagans; broken idols
William of Norwich	child crucified; cross and nails; hammer and nails
Winefred	own head in hands before altar; sword; palm branch; book
Withburga	2 does at feet; church in hand
Wulfstan, Wulstan or Wolstan	dressed as bishop; fixing crozier in tomb (of St Edmund); devil with book; giving sight to blind man
Zita, Citha or Sitha	as housekeeper; keys; loaves; rosary; bag; pitcher; basket

ATTRIBUTES & ALLEGORY
Saints

EVANGELISTS
As saints, the four gospel writers may have several attributes, but where they are given prominence as evangelists one only is usual.

Matthew	Mark	Luke	John
winged man	winged lion	winged ox	eagle

ANGELIC ORDERS
Archangels

Gabriel	the messenger of God (therefore in scenes of the Annunciation)
Michael	chief archangel; weighs souls; expulsion of Adam and Eve from Eden; killing a dragon
Raphael	the Guardian Angel, shown with Tobias and his fish
Uriel	most obscure of the Archangels, sometimes known as the Regent of the Sun, shown holding the sun; carries a book or scroll; almost never shown without the other 3 archangels.

Angels	one pair of wings; halo; holding scrolls, instruments of the Passion or musical instruments.
Cherubim	depicted with heads only and 6 wings; wings may be be strewn with eyes; may be depicted as warriors or judges; conventionally painted blue.
Seraphim	as Cherubim but painted red.
Thrones	scarlet wheels with wings, sometimes strewn with eyes.
Prophets	Amos, Daniel, Ezekiel, Habakkuk, Haggai, Hosea, Isaiah, Jeremiah, Joel, Jonah, Malachi, Micah, Nahum, Obadiah, Zechariah, Zephaniah.

LATIN DOCTORS
The medieval church recognised 4 principal scholars of the church.

Augustine	dressed as bishop or doctor
Ambrose	dressed as bishop
Gregory	dressed as pope
Jerome	dressed as cardinal

HOLY ORDERS
Each of the Holy Orders has its own characteristic dress or habit. Saints who were also monks or prelates are often depicted wearing the dress of their order and/or rank.

Benedictine — black habit *Benedict; Boniface; Thomas à Becket*
Carmelite — white cloak over brown habit (since 1297) *John de Matha, with blue/red cross on breast, fetters or angel leading captives*
Carthusian — white habit *Hugh of Lincoln, with swan and 3 flowers*
Cistercian — white or grey habit *Bernard of Clairvaux, with 3 crowns*
Dominican — white tunic, black cloak with hood (monks and nuns) *Dominic, with star on forehead and 2 dogs carrying torches; Peter the Martyr, with wound in head; Thomas Aquinas, with chalice and star on breast*
Franciscan — brown or grey habit *Francis of Assisi, with birds or animals; Anthony of Padua, with infant Christ; Louis IX, with crown of thorns*
Knights Templar — white wool habit with red cross
Knights of St John — long full black tunic with white cross on breast (red surcoat for high ranks)
Martyrs — palm frond
Hermits — T-shaped staff; rosary
Pilgrims — hat with shell; staff; wallet
Founders — model of church or monastery in hand
Abbots and Bishops — pastoral staff or crozier
Archbishops — dressed in pall *Boniface; Augustine of Canterbury; Thomas à Becket*
Popes — triple tiara; cope; pallium; triple cross in hand
Cardinals — red hat; red cloak; red robe *Jerome*

KINGS
Kings and Queens are usually richly dressed and crowned
Kings
Edmund; Edward the Confessor; Oswald; Louis IX
Queens
Helen; Frideswide; Elizabeth of Hungary
Emperor
holding imperial standard or Labarum (see p. 28) bearing cross and Chi Rho symbol
Constantine the Great

19

ATTRIBUTES & ALLEGORY
The Bible

BIBLICAL SCENES
Certain scenes, stories and themes from the Bible are often represented, sometimes with titles. There are many variations, but some of the commonest scenes described in a series of respresentations are indicated here.

Types and Antitypes
Types *(Old Testament incidents)* are often balanced by or used to foreshadow antitypes *(New Testament incidents)* in Christian decoration. Jonah was trapped in the whale for 3 days, for example, the same period of time as Christ's entombment, and the two scenes often appear together to symbolise the Resurrection. The scenes in the windows of King's College Chapel, Cambridge are a type/antitype scheme.

NEW TESTAMENT
The Passion Cycle
Entry into Jerusalem; Last Supper; Washing of the Disciples' feet; Agony in the Garden; Betrayal; Denial of Peter; Trial of Christ; Mocking of Christ; Flagellation; Crowning with Thorns; Ecce Homo; Stations of the Cross; Road to Calvary; Christ stripped of his Garments; Raising of the Cross; Crucifixion *(Virgin Mary and John or Virgin Mary and soldier, Longinus, with lance to Christ's right, John and Stephaton, with reed and sponge, to His left)*; Descent from the Cross; Pieta *(Virgin Mary supporting dead Christ);* Joseph of Arimathea removing nails and taking Body for burial; Entombment; Resurrection; 3 Maries at the Tomb; Mary Magdalene encountering Christ at Tomb *(noli me tangere)*; Journey to Emmaus; Supper at Emmaus (with two disciples); Incredulity of Thomas; Ascension; Descent of the Holy Ghost.

The Stations of the Cross
Jesus condemned to death; Jesus receives the Cross; Jesus falls under the Cross; Jesus meets the Virgin Mary; Simon of Cyrene bears the Cross; Veronica wipes the face of Jesus; Jesus falls for the second time; Jesus meets the women of Jerusalem; Jesus falls for the third time; Jesus is stripped of His garments; Jesus is nailed to the Cross; Jesus dies on the Cross; Jesus is taken down from the Cross; The body of Jesus is laid in the sepulchre.

The Life of the Virgin
Joachim and Anne, *(parents of the Virgin);* Nativity; Presentation in the Temple; Marriage; Annunciation; Visitation *(meeting of Mary and Elizabeth)*; Death; Assumption; Coronation.
The Virgin also appears in other scenes:
Nativity; Adoration of the Shepherds; Adoration of the Magi; Circumcision of Christ; Presentation in the Temple *(prophecy of Simeon);* Flight into Egypt; Descent from the Cross; Portrait being painted by St. Luke.

Miracles and Parables
Marriage at Cana *(changing water into wine);* Feeding of the 4000 *(with 7 loaves and a few fishes);* Feeding of the 5000 *(with 5 loaves and 2 fishes);* Raising of Lazarus from the Dead; Miraculous Draught of Fishes; Sermon on the Mount *(The Beatitudes);* Return of the Prodigal Son; The Good Shepherd; The Good Samaritan; and so on.

OLD TESTAMENT

The Creation; Adam and Eve; Noah building the Ark; The Flood; The Sacrifice of Isaac; Moses and the Burning Bush; Samson killing a lion or the Philistine; Moses striking the Rock; Joshua and the Walls of Jericho; Jonah and the Whale; Jacob's Ladder; Joseph and the Coat of Many Colours; David and Goliath; The Judgement of Solomon; Solomon and the Queen of Sheba; Ruth gleaning the corn; etc. etc.

APOCRYPHA

Tobias and the Angel; Judith and Holofernes; Susanna and the Elders.

TEXTS

The same biblical texts were repeatedly used in inscriptions and wall paintings. Their usual sources are the King James Authorised Version of the Bible, the Latin Bible (Vulgate), the Book of Common Prayer or the Roman Catholic Missal.

Ave Maria, Creed, Sanctus	Book of Common Prayer
The Beatitudes	Matthew, chap. V to VII
The Fruits of the Spirit	Paul's Letter to the Galatians, chap. V
The Gifts of the Holy Spirit	Isaiah, chap. XI
The Magnificat	Luke, chap. I, vv. 46 to 55
Words from the Cross	Luke, chap. XXIII, vv. 34,43,46; John, chap. XIX, vv.26-28,30; Matthew, chap. XXVII, vv.46

ALLEGORICAL SYMBOLS FROM THE OLD TESTAMENT

Altar of sacrifice or burnt offering	old testament worship
Apple	Fall of Man
Ark of the Covenant	presence of God
Bullock and censer	Day of Atonement
Butterflies	escape of soul to afterlife
Caterpillars	man's earthly life
Distaff	destiny of Eve
Doorposts and lintel	God's protection at Passover
Dove with olive branch	peace and forgiveness
Dragon	Satan; sin; pestilence
Dragon (underfoot)	victory of good over evil
Flaming sword held by angel or Hand of God	expulsion of Adam from Eden
Grapes	entry into Canaan
Lamb (paschal lamb)	Feast of Passover
Lash & bricks	captivity of Israel
Lizards, beetles, snails	transience of life and decay of the body
Scroll	Torah or 5 books of Moses
Scroll & sheaf of wheat	Pentecost
Serpent	Satan
Serpent coiled around world	sinful nature of mankind
Serpent eating tail	serpent of eternity
Seven-branch candlestick (Menorah)	old testament worship
Spade	destiny of Adam

Characters' attributes

Aaron	censer; flowering wand or rod in hand
Abel	crook; lamb
Abraham	knife; shield
Amos	crook
Cain	plough
Daniel	ram with four horns
David	harp; lion
Deborah	crown
Elijah	fiery chariot; wheel of chariot; ravens
Esau	bow and arrows
Ezekiel	closed gate
Gideon	pitcher concealing torch
Hosea	cast-off mantle
Isaac	cross formed of bundles of wood
Isaiah	saw; book; scroll
Jacob and family	sun, moon and 12 stars
Jeremiah	large stone
Jonah	whale
Joseph	coat of many colours
Joshua	trumpet; sword
Melchisedek	loaf and chalice
Micah	temple on mountain
Moses	bullrush basket; burning bush; horns; tablets
Nahum	feet appearing from cloud above mountain
Noah	ark; oar; dove with olive branch
Ruth	ear of wheat
Samson	jawbone of ass; pillars; wrestling with lion; head in lap of Delilah
Seth	thread wound 3 times around thumb
Solomon	temple (model of)
Zephaniah	sword over Jerusalem

Magi

Caspar	old man with long beard (often represents Europe)
Melchoir	middle aged man with short beard (often represents Asia)
Balthazar	young man; shown as a negro (for Africa) when the Magi represent the three continents.

Early decorators of churches used a whole series of symbols which had specific meanings for worshippers and clergy. Symbols can be confusing and need to be read in the right context. An eagle, for example, apart from being an attribute of St John the Evangelist, can also signify magnanimity or the Resurrection, and secularly the sense of Sight.

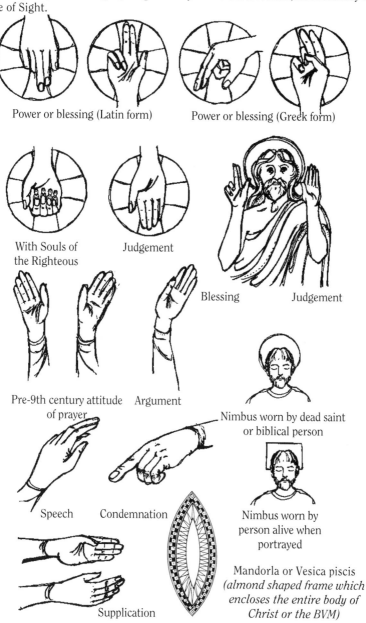

Power or blessing (Latin form)

Power or blessing (Greek form)

With Souls of the Righteous

Judgement

Blessing

Judgement

Pre-9th century attitude of prayer

Argument

Nimbus worn by dead saint or biblical person

Speech

Condemnation

Nimbus worn by person alive when portrayed

Supplication

Mandorla or Vesica piscis *(almond shaped frame which encloses the entire body of Christ or the BVM)*

ATTRIBUTES & ALLEGORY
Symbols

Stars

Seven Gifts of the
Spirit (see p 29)

Nine Fruits of the
Spirit

Twelve tribes of
Israel

Regeneration

Creator

Epiphany

Sacred Monograms

Chi Rho
*(the first 2 letters of
the Greek word for
Christ XPICTOC)*

IHC or IHS
*(the first letters of
the Greek spelling
of Jesus IHOCYC)*

Jesus Christ Victor
*N = nika (victor) or
nostra (our)*

Alpha and Omega
first and last letters of
the Greek alphabet
*(Beginning and End of
all things)*

Chi Rho with
Alpha and Omega
in a circle *(symbol
of Christ within
symbol for
eternity)*

Alpha Mu Omega
*yesterday, today
and evermore*

The Cornerstone

24

SYMBOLS OF THE HOLY TRINITY

Trefoil

Triquetra

Interlocking
Traingles

Circle within Triangle

Interwoven Circles

Triquetra and
Circle

Trinity Star or Star
of David

Holy Trinity

Equilateral
Triangle

The Three Fishes

The Three Hares

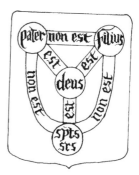

Shield with Doctrine of
the Blessed Trinity

Triangle in Circle

Cruciform or three-rayed
nimbus worn by the Trinity

ATTRIBUTES & ALLEGORY
Symbols

SYMBOLS OF THE PASSION CYCLE

 Crown of Thorns

 Sponge on Reed

 Nails

 Thirty Pieces of Silver

 Scourges

 Hammer and Pincers

 Dice and Seamless Robe

 The Cock that Crowed

 Cross with shroud or winding sheet

 Pillar and Cords

 The Title from Iesus Nazarene Rex Iudacorum (*Jesus of Nazareth, King of the Jews*)

 Fist that buffeted Him

 Lantern

 Jug of Vinegar

 Five Wounds

 Agony in Gethsemane

 Ladder

 Sword and Staff

Seven Lamps or Seven Flames

Seven Doves

The Holy Spirit
The Dove

Agnus Dei with
Book of Seven Seals

Agnus Dei with
Banner of Victory

The Pelican in her Piety
*(the pelican piercing its breast to feed its
young with its blood is a symbol of Christ's
sacrifice on the cross).*

The Greek word for fish signifies
Jesus Christ Son of God, Saviour

Paschal Lamb
Old Testament

ATTRIBUTES & ALLEGORY

27

ATTRIBUTES & ALLEGORY
Symbols

SYMBOLS OF THE BLESSED VIRGIN MARY (BVM)

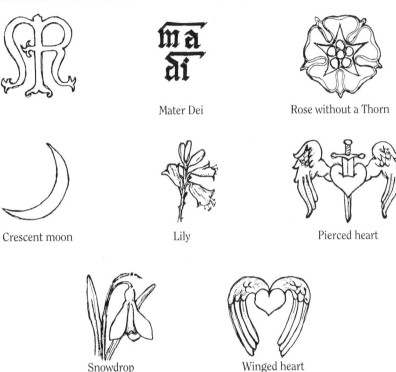

Mater Dei

Rose without a Thorn

Crescent moon

Lily

Pierced heart

Snowdrop

Winged heart

SYMBOLS OF POWER

Temporal figures may carry a staff of office or a specific symbol signifying power and authority. Archibishops, bishops and abbots may carry a croizier or pastoral staff. The pastoral staff will be carried in the right hand except during benediction when it will be in the left hand. On the eve of battle in 312 AD Constantine saw in a dream a cross in the sky, and heard a voice saying "In hoc signo vinces," *(By this sign shalt thou conquer)*. It is said after that he substituted the Chi Rho emblem for the Roman eagle on the standard, or labarum, of the legions.

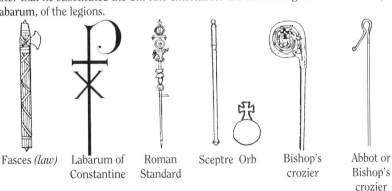

Fasces *(law)*   Labarum of Constantine   Roman Standard   Sceptre   Orb   Bishop's croizier   Abbot or Bishop's croizier

GROUPS OF SEVEN
Seven is the symbolic number of perfection.

Gifts of the Holy Spirit
Wisdom
Understanding
Counsel
Fortitude
Knowledge
True Godliness/Piety
Fear of the Lord

Liberal Arts
(sometimes accompanied by virtues)
Arithmetic
Astronomy
Geometry
Grammar
Logic
Music
Rhetoric

Sacraments
Baptism
Confirmation
Communion (Eucharist)
Penance (Confession)
Holy Orders
Matrimony
Extreme Unction

Vices or Deadly Sins
Anger
Covetousness
Envy
Gluttony
Lust
Pride
Sloth

Virtues (generally female)

Faith	holding a cross; chalice; foot resting on a square stone block
Hope	holding an anchor; eyes and hands raised to Heaven; sometimes with wings
Charity	nursing a child; surrounded by children or holding vase with flames; holding a flaming heart
Justice	scales; sword; blindfold
Prudence	holding a snake and mirror; sometimes with two faces looking in both directions simultaneously, sometimes the snake is a dragon
Temperance	pouring liquid from one vessel to another *(watering the wine)*; sheathed sword; two vases
Fortitude	dressed in armour resembling Minerva; sword; club; shield; broken pillar; lion

COSTUME
Biblical

100 BC - 100 AD

Depictions in mediaeval or later churches may be based upon fairly accurate knowledge of what was worn in a specific area or date or may, especially in late coloured glass window lights, be the invention of the artist.

The drawings which illustrate pages 30 and 31 show the type of garments worn in the century before the birth of Christ and up to 200 AD. Although we do not possess actual items of dress, with the exception of leather and metal footwear, belts and armour and the Bronze Age woollen garments preserved in Danish peat bogs, our knowledge of what was worn is fairly accurate. It comes from the written word, Tacitus for example, from sculpture, metal and stone relief-work and from wall and tomb paintings. These drawings are an accurate depiction from these sources.

Garments worn in this period were not fitted to the figure, such skill only developed during the Middle Ages. The amount of seam sewing and the fabric and decoration used varied according to the area; this was affected by climate, religion and local custom. For example, Hebrew garments, though loose, shapeless and worn in layers, were sewn at the sides and shoulders and had sleeves. Persian dress was also sewn. We owe the introduction of the coat to the Persians. The classical dress of Greece and Rome, in contrast, was draped, largely unsewn and held to the body by belts and brooches. It consisted of rectangles of fabric for tunics, gowns and cloaks.

1. Persian dress wearing long coat over belted tunic, trousers and shoes. Curled beard and hair. 2. Hebrew dress. Tunics (kethoneth) with shawl (tallith) on top. The tassels (tsitsith) have religious significance.

7. Greek hairstyle
8. Roman hairstyle

3. Persian shoe

4. Roman sandal

12, 13. Roman draped dress 1st century AD. The man wears leather, laced boots.

5. Persian linen headdress

6. Hebrew turban

9, 10. Greek draped costume 1st century BC. Fastened to figure by girdles and shoulder brooches.

11. Roman lady's coiffure

Drawings by Doreen Yarwood Encyclopedia of World Costume, Batsford

1ST TWO CENTURIES AD
1-2 British   3-5 Franks and Gauls

The dress shown on this page reflects that worn in Europe at this time. We have detailed understanding of such attire, partly from written records, accounts such as *The Agricola* and *The Germania* written AD 98 by the Roman historian Cornelius Tacitus, also from sculptured reliefs, notably those on the columns of Trajan (AD 114) and Marcus Aurelius (AD 174) in Rome. A life-size replica of the former is on display in the Victoria and Albert Museum in London. Apart from Spain, the colder climate of much of Europe compared with the Middle East, necessitated wearing warmer clothes. In the climate of Greece and Rome fine linens, pleated fabrics and imported silks were available and styles were sophisticated (page 30). In northern Europe the chief textile was wool with fur linings. Garments were loose but sewn. Shoes, if worn, were of untanned hide. Legs were bare or trousered. These latter were loose and shapeless, tied at waist and ankle with drawstring.

6-7 Spain 8-10 Teutonic tribesman

Drawings by Doreen Yarwood *European Costume*, Batsford

COSTUME
Early Middle Ages Up to 1340

2. Surcoat & coif, 1245

4. Surcoat, hood, liripipe 1310

5. Hood, liripipe 1340

1. Tabard c. 1200

3. Gardecorps, 1270

Throughout this period garments were still loose and ill-fitting, sewn only down the side seams. Men wore ankle-or knee-length tunics, women gowns, both were cut similarly. Back and front of the garment were cut in one piece with a round hole made for the head. There were thus no shoulder seams or set-in sleeves, the sleeves being cut in one with the garment leaving wide armholes. Fabrics were chiefly wool and linen though, as a result of the Crusades, increased trade brought importation of richer fabrics from Italy and the East for the wealthy. 13th century dress was noted for its extreme simplicity of line and lack of decoration. During this century the **surcoat** (surcote) was introduced. It began as a tabard, a simple, unsewn garment originating as a covering for the armour of the Crusading knight in order to conceal the sun's glare on the metal. The tabard slowly developed into the longer, sleeveless surcoat worn by both sexes. Later, long, open sleeves were introduced (**gardecorps**). Underwear, (both sexes) comprised a long linen shirt or chemise and knee-length long shapeless underpants held by a drawstring at the waist (**braies**). These were tucked into cloth stockings and gartered. Men wore a linen cap (**coif**) and, on top, a hat or, more commonly, a hood with shoulder cape. After 1300 the point on top lengthened into a long tail (**liripipe**). Women's long hair was plaited in coils and encased in a net. This could be accompanied by a draped gorget (**wimple**) and/or chin band (**barbette**) and cap, all in white linen.

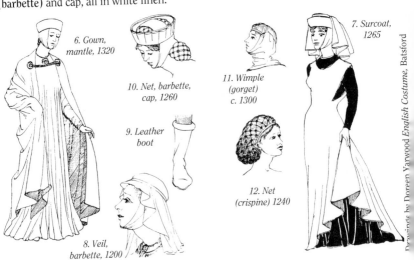

6. Gown, mantle, 1320

7. Surcoat, 1265

10. Net, barbette, cap, 1260

11. Wimple (gorget) c. 1300

9. Leather boot

12. Net (crispine) 1240

8. Veil, barbette, 1200

Drawings by Doreen Yarwood English Costume, Batsford

1. Fur-trimmed velvet sideless surcoat, 1360

2. Parti-coloured tunic & hose, 1350

3. 1365

4. Houppelande, 1415

5. Chaperon, 1455

After 1340 dress changed radically. Man had learned to tailor and clothes cut and sewn to fit the figure were made. Both masculine tunic and feminine gown were cut in four sections and seamed at front, back and sides. Sleeves were inset. Men's tunics of 1350 were hip-length with a hip belt. Gradually they became shorter and shorter. To complement this, hose became longer and braies shorter. Hose then became tights with a bag at the fork (**codpiece**). They were of fabric, not knitted and were seamed in four sections. The tunic and gowns were waisted (**cotehardie**). Ladies wore a full surcoat on top. Then, suited to the older and less slender, came the loose houppelande worn by both sexes. Decoration became rich and varied: parti-colouring; dagged edges; fur trimming. Fabrics became richer: velvets; satins; brocade. The masculine hood became a padded roll with liripipe (**chaperon**). Tall hats were fashionable. Ladies' headdresses took many elaborate forms: wired cauls; heart-shaped designs; horned shapes. Veils accompanied most headdresses. Hair was completely hidden.

6. Padded long tunic, 1450

7. Houppelande, 1435

8. Houppelande, 1445

9. Young man of fashion, 1450

Drawings by Doreen Yarwood *European Costume*, published Batsford

COSTUME
Spread of the Renaissance 1465 - 1540

1. Gown, 1475

2. Gable hood, 1500

3. 1520

4. c. 1495

5. Fashionable youth, 1505

Costume, no less than the other arts of mankind, reflects current events and important movements. The Renaissance, which had begun much earlier in Italy, by this time had brought its cult of Humanism to northern Europe. The effects could be seen in close-fitting male garments intended to display the human figure; this was evidenced especially in the hose, very short tunics, long hair and swashbuckling hats (5). Young men, in particular, followed such fashions, older men were more discreet (1). The Reformation began to show its effect on dress in the early 16th century in a greater covering up of the figure and use of heavier materials (9). For ladies, the Spanish **farthingale** made its appearance. This was a canvas underskirt reinforced by circular whalebone hoops extending from waist to ground. It was accompanied by strict corseting to provide a slender waist and uplifted breasts (6). A variety of feminine hoods developed from the late 15th century steeple headdress (7, 8, 10).

6. Farthingale gown, 1535

8. Gable hood, 1515

7. Steeple headdress, 1470

10. Gable hood, 1536

11. 1515

12. Velvet shoe

9. 1530

from Doreen Yarwood *European Costume*, Batsford

34

1. Farthingale, French hood c 1547

2. Princess Mary c 1545

3. Ruff, doublet, trunk hose, 1580

4. Queen Elizabeth c 1590

Fashion in dress has always been set and practised by the wealthy, important section of society. In a wider context it has been the nations which, at any given time, were the most powerful which initiated the mode. In the years 1540 - 1620 the dominant country was Spain. From here came the **cape**, the **doublet**, the **trunk hose** and the **ruff**, the **corset** and **farthingale**. Never before or since, has fashionable dress been so rich, so be-jewelled and embroidered. It was overseas exploration and the discovery of the New World which brought these riches and influence. Not only was the costume richly decorative but the fashion was to mould the human figure to an artificial form by bombast and restriction. Men wore corsets and padded their doublets and trunk hose; women wore ever-wider farthingales and tighter corsets. Both sexes displayed starched and supported cartwheel ruffs. Relaxation only began to appear from about 1610.

COSTUME

Fashion of the Western World, Batsford

5. Making music 1611
Spinet and lute
More natural, less restrictive garments

COSTUME
Elegance and naturalism 1620 - 1660

*1. Dashing cavalier,
1630 - 5*

*2. Mrs Tradescant.
Puritan hat and cap. 1645*

3. Charles I, 1638-40

*4. Queen Henrietta
Maria, 1635-40*

*5. Prince Charles
c 1636*

By 1620 the pendulum of fashion had swung sharply away from restriction and bombast. Spanish influence waned and the centre of importance had moved to the Low Countries which continued to be the dominant factor until France, under Louis XIV, began its long reign over fashion in the 1660s. Professor Randolph Schwabe, late Director of the Slade College of Art, once described the dress of the years 1620 - 60 as 'long locks, lace and leather'. With reference to masculine dress this was particularly apt. It was an age of elegance, long hair (natural, not a wig) plumed Cavalier hats, a large lace collar to replace the ruff, jacket and breeches and those superbly soft leather boots, their open buckets tops frothing with lace boot hose. Ladies' dress was less impressive but on similar lines: corset and farthingale had gone. In England the Puritan version of the style was basically the same theme but stripped of all decoration and lace, a tall black hat replacing the plumed one.

*6-12. Portrait of a Flemish family c 1655-60.
Children dressed as miniatures
of their parents.*

Drawings by Doreen Yarwood European Costume, Batsford

1. William III, Periwig, 1700

3. Lady's shoe

4. Gentleman's shoe

2. Queen Mary, 1694

5. & 6. 1665

COSTUME

Men's dress in the 1660s (6) continued to be elegant and comfortable . The jacket became much shorter to display a full white shirt finished at the neck with a lace-edged cravat. This was the era of petticoat breeches (correctly termed **rhinegraves** after the Count of that name who popularised them). They were very full, long shorts decorated by rows of ribbon loops. Hair was still long and flowing. Later in the 1660s came the introduction of the open coat (9). This garment originated in Persia (page 30(1)). By 1680 the coat had become waisted and buttoned. It had large cuffs, but no collar due to the wig covering, and frogged decoration (7). Before the end of the century the multi-curled periwig had supplanted natural flowing hair (1, 7, 9). By this time ladies' dress had begun its slow return to corsetry to achieve a slender waist but, as yet, no framework petticoats. Tall wired lace headdresses echoed the male piled-up periwig curls (2).

7. Gentleman, 1695

9. Early style of coat, 1665

8. Lady with parasol, 1689

COSTUME
France: Arbiter of Fashion 1715 - 1760

1. English gentleman, 1735-45

2. Pig-tail wig, 1740

3. Tie wig c 1730

4. Black tricorne hat, 1750

5. Lavender taffeta gown, 1755-60

In these years France's dominant role was undisputed. In all the trades and skills essential to *la mode* she had built up total pre-eminence from dressmaking to haberdashery, textiles to corsetry. The French language was that of Europe's ruling class. In men's dress the 3-piece suit (forerunner of that of the 1930s) - coat, waistcoat, breeches - was now established. Coat and breeches were often of matching fabric and decoration; in contrast, the waistcoat would be richly embroidered or brocaded all over (1, 9). The now much smaller wig was powdered white with rice or wheatmeal with unfortunate livestock accompaniment. It was surmounted by the hat of the age: the **tricorne**. For ladies the framework petticoat was back, this time in hoop design or, as the French called it, **le panier** *(basket)*. In designs of the 1720s and 1730s the gown was loose-fitting, the rear falling in box pleats to ground level. By the 1750s the tightly-corseted waist was again marked, the gown elaborately decorated with ruffles and bows.

6. Portrait young girl, 1715

7. & 8. Painting by de Troy of French dress, 1728-31

9. Actual garments, Paris, 1738

Drawings by Doreen Yarwood *European Costume*, Batsford

38

Artificial Extremism to Revolutionary Change 1760 - 1800

1. Actual dress, 1799

2. Actual dress, 1795

4. Hoop skirt, 1770

3. Portrait, 1790

5. Actual costume, 1775

Styles of dress under French influence, especially for women, became more and more artificial in shape, less and less comfortable as the 18th century progressed. Corsets were tight, hooped skirts wide (4), gowns overdecorated and, most artificial of all, women adapted tall wigs as men had done nearly a century earlier but these were powdered and, often, ridiculously overdecorated (7, 8). Meanwhile, in England, simpler, more elegant styles of dress were evolving for both sexes and this **mode a l'anglaise**, as it was called, began to influence all of Europe except France. It is typified in portraits by Gainsborough and his colleagues (6-9). With the French Revelution came ideas of democracy and the origins in ancient Greece. Draped long skirts, thin fabrics, décolleté necklines and high waistlines replaced artificiality.

6-9. Actual costumes, 1789-90

6.

7.

8.

9.

Drawings by Doreen Yarwood *European Costume*, Batsford

COSTUME

COSTUME
Military

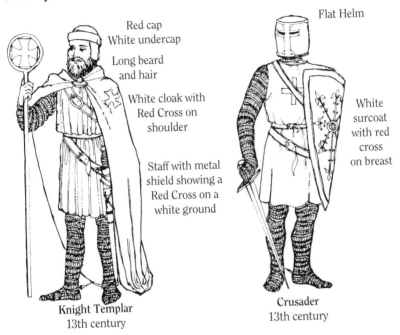

Red cap
White undercap

Long beard
and hair

White cloak with
Red Cross on
shoulder

Staff with metal
shield showing a
Red Cross on a
white ground

Knight Templar
13th century

Flat Helm

White
surcoat
with red
cross
on breast

Crusader
13th century

Morion helmet

Sleeveless jerkin

Doublet

Sash worn over Cuirass

Swordbelt

Breeches

Musket

Hose

Thighboots

Soldier
c. 1590

Knights in armour are found on tombs and memorial brasses and individual pieces of armour may be depicted on all manner of decoration. Genuine armour and firearms were stored in churches and some may still be found over tombs, although often mixed up and put on the wrong tombs over the centuries.
(See MONUMENTS: Brasses)

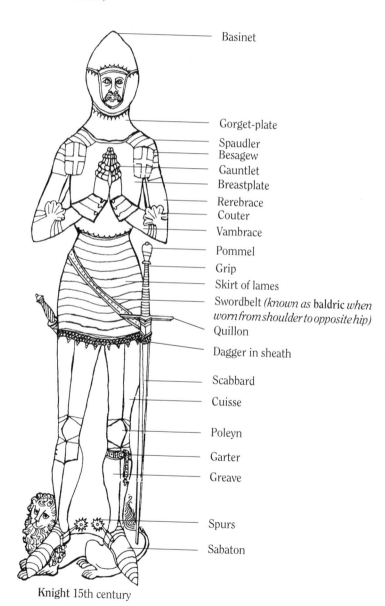

Basinet

Gorget-plate

Spaudler
Besagew

Gauntlet

Breastplate

Rerebrace
Couter

Vambrace

Pommel

Grip

Skirt of lames

Swordbelt *(known as* **baldric** *when worn from shoulder to opposite hip)*
Quillon

Dagger in sheath

Scabbard

Cuisse

Poleyn

Garter

Greave

Spurs

Sabaton

Knight 15th century

COSTUME

Arms and Armour

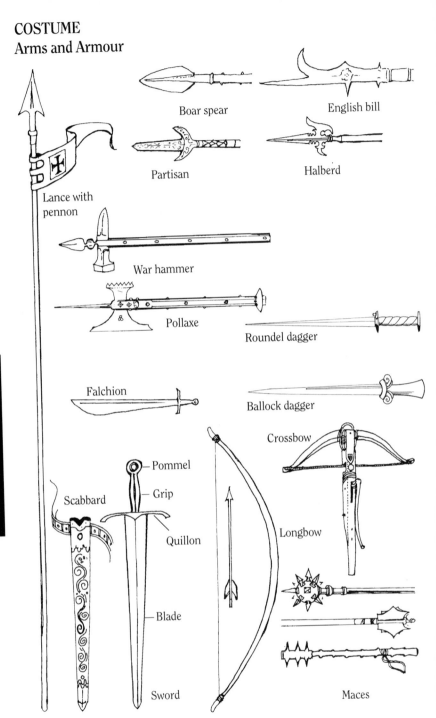

Boar spear

English bill

Partisan

Halberd

Lance with pennon

War hammer

Pollaxe

Roundel dagger

Falchion

Ballock dagger

Crossbow

Pommel

Grip

Scabbard

Quillon

Longbow

Blade

Sword

Maces

COSTUME
Arms and Armour

HELMETS

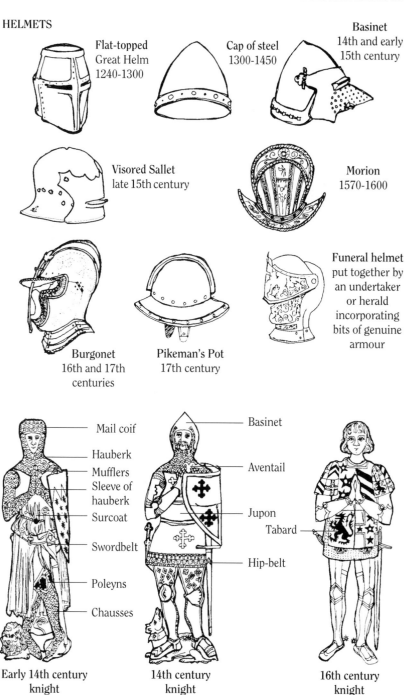

Flat-topped
Great Helm
1240-1300

Cap of steel
1300-1450

Basinet
14th and early
15th century

Visored Sallet
late 15th century

Morion
1570-1600

Burgonet
16th and 17th
centuries

Pikeman's Pot
17th century

Funeral helmet
put together by
an undertaker
or herald
incorporating
bits of genuine
armour

Mail coif

Hauberk

Mufflers
Sleeve of
hauberk

Surcoat

Swordbelt

Poleyns

Chausses

Basinet

Aventail

Jupon

Tabard

Hip-belt

Early 14th century
knight

14th century
knight

16th century
knight

COSTUME

43

COSTUME
Vestments

Alb	full length belted white tunic with narrow sleeves. Nowadays it is impossible to distinguish Anglican from Roman Catholic albs. Sometimes embroidered at hem or trimmed with lace flounce and cuffs.
Almuce	cape or scarf with hood, sometimes made of fur, or fur lined.
Amice	white linen neck-cloth sometimes with an apparel at one edge.
Apparel	decorated panel applied to albs and amices. Not found on 20th century albs but may be seen on early ones in stained glass, paintings and brasses. Although seen with dalmatics, apparels are not fixed to dalmatics and are only fixed to the centre top of amices and, many years ago, to alb cuffs and hems front and back.
Biretta	black, purple, red or white ridged hat, worn according to rank by priest, bishop, cardinal or pope.
Cassock	full length sleeved gown, single or double breasted, black or coloured according to rank.
Chasuble	circular or oval cape with central head opening and **orphreys**; the principal vestment worn by an officiating priest. Full tent-like chasuble often known as **romanesque**.
Chimere	long sleeveless gown worn over the rochet
Clavi	decorative woven or embroidered bands found on early tunics and dalmatics.
Cope	semicircular cape fastened with a **morse**, decorated with a hood and orphreys. 20th century copes are often hand-worked in combinations of kid-leather, beads, jewels, metallic threads, cords and stitchery, incorporating a variety of symbols (see p. 156 for sample description).
Dalmatic	sleeved open-sided tunic, worn by deacons, decorated with stripes called **clavi** and sometimes with apparels.
Girdle	white or coloured cord belt with tassels.
Hood (academic)	worn by graduates in colours according to type of University degree.
Hood (cope)	flat vestigial hood attached at back of cope.
Lappets	pair of ribands *(ribbons)* attached at back of mitre.
Maniple	decorated band worn over the left arm, resembling a short stole, originally a towel
Mitre	peaked headdress worn by bishops, popes and abbots: simplex = white; aurifrigiata = gold or silver on white; pretiosa = jewelled.
Morse	clasp or fastening on the cope, often made of precious metals, enamelled and set with jewels. Can also be an embroidered band. Originally metal only worn by a Bishop, fabric for others.
Mozetta	short hooded cape, buttoned down front, coloured as rank.
Orphrey	embroidered band, usually applied, found on chasubles and copes. On altar frontals, orphreys are decorative panels, loose or attached.
Pallium or Pall	originally a woollen vestment worn by archbishops, usually shown as a narrow Y-shaped strip with embroidered crosses, falling down the centre front and back.

COSTUME

Pastoral staff or Crozier	stave carried by high dignitaries on which may be a cross, crook or horizontal crook (**Tau stave**); sometimes a **vexillium** *(scarf)* is attached.
Rochet	similar to alb but shorter, either sleeveless or sleeves gathered at wrist.
Stole	decorated band worn round the neck, beneath the chasuble, resembling, but longer than, the maniple, usually with a device at each end and a cross at the neck.
Surplice	white gown, differing from the alb by long flowing sleeves, worn unbelted over the cassock.
Tiara	headdress of a pope.
Tunicle	similar to dalmatic, although longer when worn by bishops with a dalmatic; it has narrow sleeves and no apparels except occasionally near the neck; it is usually worn by sub-deacons.

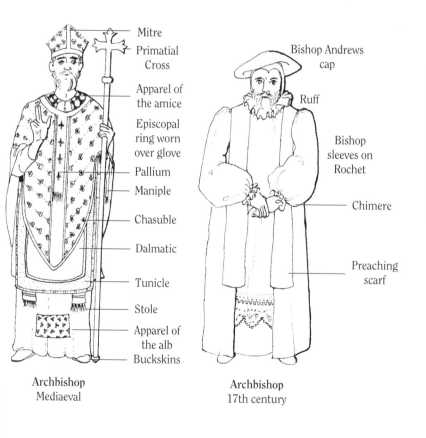

Mitre
Primatial Cross
Apparel of the amice
Episcopal ring worn over glove
Pallium
Maniple
Chasuble
Dalmatic
Tunicle
Stole
Apparel of the alb
Buckskins

Bishop Andrews cap
Ruff
Bishop sleeves on Rochet
Chimere
Preaching scarf

Archbishop
Mediaeval

Archbishop
17th century

COSTUME

COSTUME
Vestments

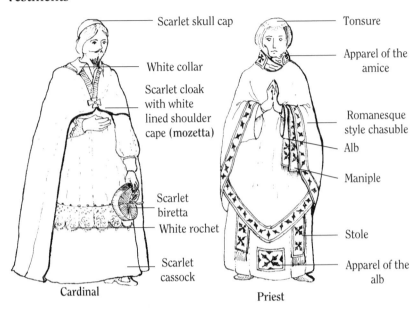

Scarlet skull cap

White collar

Scarlet cloak with white lined shoulder cape (**mozetta**)

Scarlet biretta

White rochet

Scarlet cassock

Cardinal

Tonsure

Apparel of the amice

Romanesque style chasuble

Alb

Maniple

Stole

Apparel of the alb

Priest

DALMATICS

Tassels

Clavi

Traditional Dalmatic
with tassels and clavi

Dalmatic with clavi
20th century

GOTHIC CHASUBLES
with orphreys

Y-shaped

V-shaped

Pallium-shaped

Appliqued with Chi-Rho,
Alpha and Omega,
and cross motifs

Pillar shaped

COPES

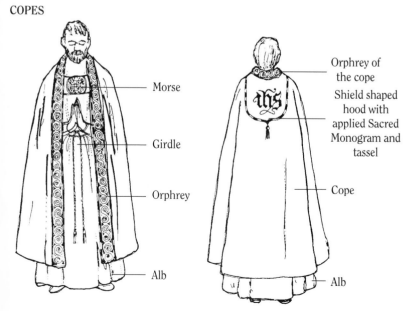

Morse

Girdle

Orphrey

Alb

Orphrey of
the cope

Shield shaped
hood with
applied Sacred
Monogram and
tassel

Cope

Alb

COSTUME
Vestments

Cope with rounded and fringed hood with hand-embroidered Maltese cross and orphreys of coloured velvet.

Lent/Advent cope with embroidered Crown of Thorns, Eclipse of the Sun and Star of Advent motifs.

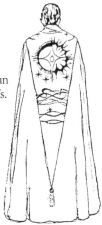

Cowl hood

Deacons' stoles	worn from left shoulder to right hip
Organists' cassocks and surplices	usually with fuller skirt for ease of movement at the organ. Surplice has semi-wing sleeves.
Preaching bands	usually 14cm - 20cm long
Preaching stoles	worn over the surplice and secured by a small chain in front, stoles are usually 127cm long. Until recently, stoles when worn over an alb were crossed at the front by priests and uncrossed by bishops. They are usually worn uncrossed today.
Preaching scarves or Tippets	usually gathered at the neck with pinked ends, can be made ungathered and/or with plain ends. Length according to height of wearer. Black for priests, blue for readers.
Vergers' gowns	can have divided sleeves and open front for maximum movement and comfort or can have a closed front with velveteen trimmings, collar and epaulettes.

Latin

Glory

Sovereignty

Calvary

Passion

Celtic

Iona

Cross & Thorny Crown

Salitre

Fimbriated

Addorned

Easter

Russian Orthodox

Lorraine

Patriarchal

Papal

St Peter's

St James's

Christus Rex

Crucifix

CROSSES

CROSSES
Terms

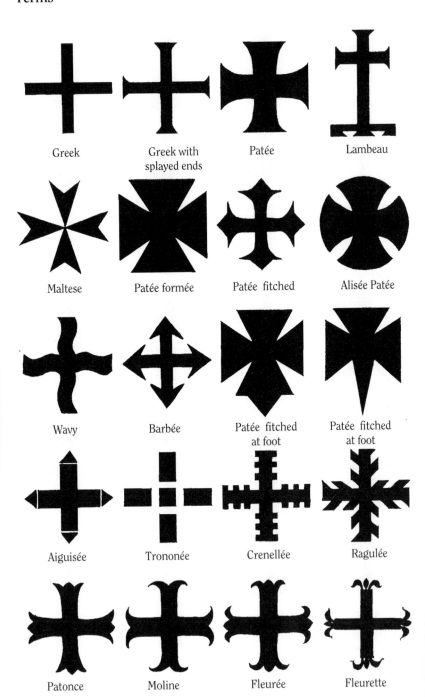

Greek

Greek with splayed ends

Patée

Lambeau

Maltese

Patée formée

Patée fitched

Alisée Patée

Wavy

Barbée

Patée fitched at foot

Patée fitched at foot

Aiguisée

Trononée

Crenellée

Ragulée

Patonce

Moline

Fleurée

Fleurette

Pommée

Bezant

Bottonée

Canterbury

Paternoster

Milrine

Clercée or
entrailed

Cercelée

Four pheons

Four ermine spots

Nebulée

St Julian's

Cross
Crosslet

Cross Crosslet
fitched

Crusader's or
Jerusalem

Cantonée

Degraded

Potent

St Chad's

Quadrate

CROSSES

51

CROSSES
Terms

Parted and frettée

Triparted

Frettée

Masclée

Fylfot or Swastika

Potent rebated

Chain

Looped

Anchor

Alpha and Omega with Anchor Cross

Y-shaped

Clavis

Latin cross fleurée

Tau

Ankh

Crux Ansata

Floriated quatrefoil

Circle and quatrefoil

Greek cross fleurée

Floriated octafoil

TERMS

Crucifix	cross with the image of Christ affixed
Crucifix of Christus Rex	crucifix with Christ figure in eucharistic vestments and crown
Christ in Agony	Crucifix figure with open eyes
Corpus Christi or The Dead Christ	crucifix figure with closed eyes

Ivory corpus Christi screwed onto oak Latin cross with bevelled edges
Bearded head, with closed eyes, crowned with thorns and bowed to the right arms
upstretched and fingers clasped; slightly curved torso with loose **perizonium** *(loin cloth)* knotted over right hip; right knee bent; feet superimposed but nailed separately.
Ivory scroll super-inscription or **titulus** attached with brass nail.

DECORATION
Friezes

Decorative friezes and motifs may appear on a variety of objects in a variety of materials as architectural mouldings, embroidery, painted decoration or carving.

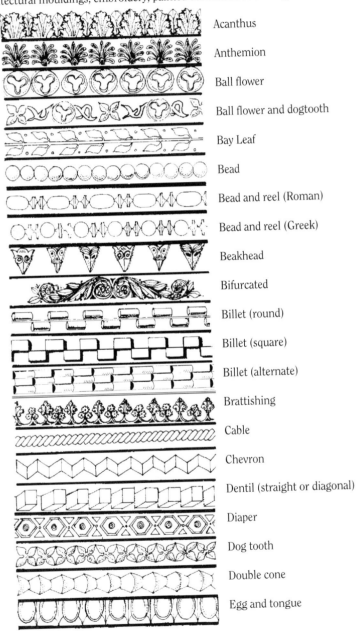

Acanthus

Anthemion

Ball flower

Ball flower and dogtooth

Bay Leaf

Bead

Bead and reel (Roman)

Bead and reel (Greek)

Beakhead

Bifurcated

Billet (round)

Billet (square)

Billet (alternate)

Brattishing

Cable

Chevron

Dentil (straight or diagonal)

Diaper

Dog tooth

Double cone

Egg and tongue

Egg and dart

Embattled

Enriched chevron

Festoon

Fleur-de-Lys

Four leaf flower

Fret or lattice or key or meander

Gadrooning, lobing or nulling

Goughing, chanelling or adzed
(usually called scoop)

Guilloche

Husk

Imbricated interrupted by Tudor
ornament

Interlacing *(resembling
strapwork and moresque)*

Knotwork

Lotus alternating with palmette

Lozenge

Lunette

Meander

Moresque *(16th century term for
interlacing)*

Nailhead

Ovolo *(convex moulding)*

DECORATION
Friezes

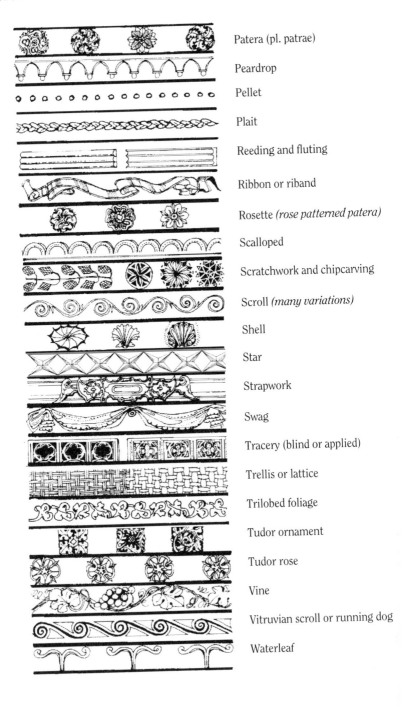

Patera (pl. patrae)

Peardrop

Pellet

Plait

Reeding and fluting

Ribbon or riband

Rosette *(rose patterned patera)*

Scalloped

Scratchwork and chipcarving

Scroll *(many variations)*

Shell

Star

Strapwork

Swag

Tracery (blind or applied)

Trellis or lattice

Trilobed foliage

Tudor ornament

Tudor rose

Vine

Vitruvian scroll or running dog

Waterleaf

 Basketwork medallion

 Grotesque

 Bucranium

 Mask

 Chinoiserie medallion

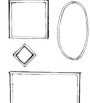 Medallions

 Cusp *(projecting point where foils meet)*

 Roundel

 Foils: trefoil quatrefoil, cinque-, sex-, etc.

 Pendant

 Foliation

 Cherub, putto or amorino

 Floriation

 Flory and counterflory

DECORATION
Flora and Fauna

Fruits, flowers, trees and figures may have symbolic meaning (see ATTRIBUTES & ALLEGORY) or may simply serve a decorative purpose.

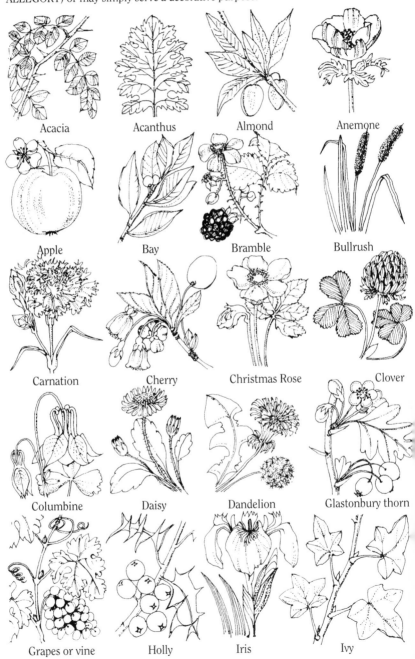

Acacia   Acanthus   Almond   Anemone

Apple   Bay   Bramble   Bullrush

Carnation   Cherry   Christmas Rose   Clover

Columbine   Daisy   Dandelion   Glastonbury thorn

Grapes or vine   Holly   Iris   Ivy

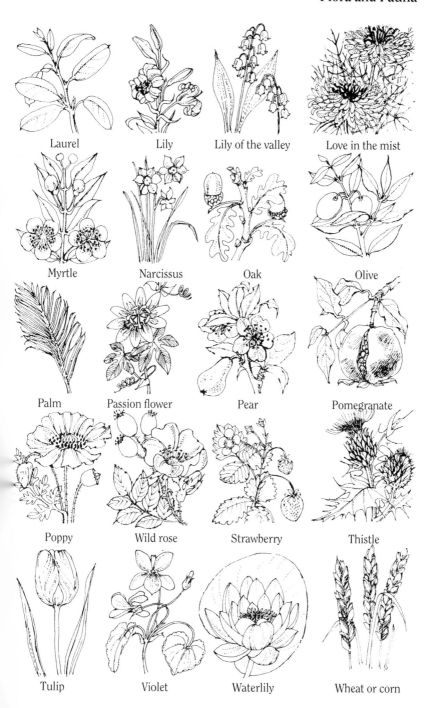

Laurel   Lily   Lily of the valley   Love in the mist

Myrtle   Narcissus   Oak   Olive

Palm   Passion flower   Pear   Pomegranate

Poppy   Wild rose   Strawberry   Thistle

Tulip   Violet   Waterlily   Wheat or corn

DECORATION
Flora and Fauna

Antelope, hind,
hart, doe or stag

Basilisk or
cockatrice

Centaur

Dragon

Wyvern

Griffin

Dolphin

Phoenix

Salamander

Unicorn

Wodehouse

Green man

Tree of Jesse
A branched tree with incorporated figures which combines the prophecy of Isaiah with the genealogical descent of Christ from Jesse (St. Matthew's Gospel, Chapter 1). The figures on the branches represent the Prophets, often in contemporary dress, and the kings of Judah in the line of David. The Blessed Virgin Mary appears near the apex, holding the Child or with the figure of Christ above her and either the descending Dove of the Holy Spirit or doves representing the Gifts of the Holy Spirit.

Tree of Life
A naturalistic representation as a symbol of life, knowledge and salvation.

Tree of life

Scroll frieze
14th century

DECORATION
Frames

Every edging, rim, border etc which encloses something is a frame. Frames are usually decorative and may be features in themselves. The same term is used for the skeleton of a piece of furniture.

Architectural frames	used for doors, windows, panels, tablets, medallions, niches, soffits, pictures, books etc.
Cartouche	frame in the shape of a scroll of parchment with turned up ends.
Frame	encloses a space with symmetrical decoration.
Partial frame	external ornament top and bottom to emphasise the vertical, the lower ornament having the general shape of a bracket and the upper making a cresting feature.
Strapwork frame	use of strapwork to surround or partially surround object; characteristic of Renaissance style, frequently with additional foliage and festoons. In books, strapwork often includes architectural forms.

Partial frame   Frame   Cartouche

Strapwork bookplate

Strapwork frame

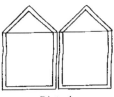 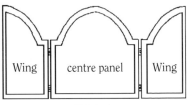

Diptych   Triptych

Wall paintings

Painted mural decoration was common in pre-Reformation churches in Britain and constantly replaced and renewed. In the mid-16th century, many wall paintings were obliterated and some were overpainted with texts (The Sentences). In the 20th century some mediaeval paintings have been restored from beneath limewashing and overpainting. Subject matter was more important than artistic merit and few painters, except those working for royalty, are known.

Fresco	painting onto damp plaster, usually employed in Italy but rarely in Britain.
Secco	painting onto dry plaster, usually in red, yellow, white and black, commonly employed in Britain. Paintings applied by this method have a tendency to flake off the wall.

Wall paintings should be read as a strip cartoon; they are sometimes in two or more tiers, the individual scenes being divided by architectural motifs or bordered top and bottom. Incidents are often telescoped so that figures at the end of one scene may be back to back with the figures in the next. Scenes are stylised. Good people have haloes; bad people are caricatured; accessories are enlarged out of proportion to emphasise rank, authority or cruelty. Costume is usually contemporary and will give a clue to the date of the work. Souls are usually naked figures but carry rank identifications *(see ATTRIBUTES & ALLEGORY)*. Subjects group into 4 types:

Decorative masonry patterns
   12th/14th centuries: scroll, chevron, heraldry, vine, diapering
   14th/15th centuries: decoration characterised by clear stencilling
Bible stories including the Tree of Life and Tree of Jesse
Saints, apostles, martyrs and scenes from their lives
Moralities or allegorical themes containing warnings against particular sins or modes of life including the Seven Deadly Sins, the Seven Works of Mercy, the Weighing of Souls and the Doom or Last Judgement.

The Doom

Christ, robed to display the Five Wounds, seated on a rainbow, judging the living and dead. He blesses with one hand and holds up an open palm of judgement with the other. His feet rest on a sphere. He is flanked by groups of the Heavenly Host, Apostles, Evangelists, the Virgin Mary and St John the Baptist. Angels bear the Symbols of the Passion or blow trumpets. **Scrolls** often bear *"Come ye blessed of my Father and inherit your Kingdom"* on His right and *"Go ye evil doers into eternal fire"* on His left. Lower down, in the general resurrection St Peter receives the Blessed at the gate of Heaven and the sinners are damned in Hell.

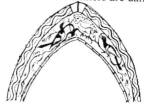

Owl and Magpie copied from a Bestiary illustrating *"idle chatterers mocking wisdom"* c.1330

Trophy *(decorative group of weapons, musical instruments or armour usually displayed with foliations, ribbons and flowers).*

DECORATION
Walls

Masons' marks

Distinguishing marks incised in stonework to identify the craftsman who worked it. Complex marks may have illustrated the pedigree of the mason, others were simple identifications for payment. Position marks indicated the order in which the stones were to be set.

Vertebrate band *(continuous design, usually of flowers, fruit or foilage with the main stem running through the centre)*

Rinceau band *(similar to vertebrate, but with a wavy central stem)*

Allegorical vine border, 13th century

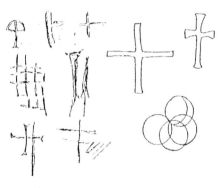

Graffiti can be inscriptions, shapes, figures, or even music, scratched or cut in the fabric or furnishings of a building. In a church they occur chiefly in stone or plaster surfaces.

Pelta or double axe pattern, c.1100

Consecration crosses, usually 12 within church (painted) and 12 without (carved)

Mediaeval graffiti may be of considerable interest and should be recorded carefully with the help of torch and magnifying glass. Take measurements, including height from the floor, and give the location and any historical information (as distinct from imaginative interpretation). Each graffito can be illustrated by a sketch, a photograph (side-lit), or a rubbing made with soft pencil. Categories often include: objects drawn for votive purposes; crosses made by pilgrims and others; a priest's name and his induction date on chancel doorways; circles and compass-drawn motifs marking sites of consecration crosses; outline drawings on which mural paintings were based; portraits and caricatures; sketches for a craftsman's work, eg. window tracery; staves of music (at points where processional singing took place).

A knowledge of the basic principles of heraldry will help in understanding monuments, stained glass windows, kneelers and embroidered banners.

Heraldic decoration can be described either by blazoning *(using correct heraldic terminology)* or tricking *(making a rough sketch with a detailed description of colours and motifs)* (see page 76). To identify a particular coat of arms it may help to look for another elsewhere in the church or graveyard under which there might be a helpful inscription. Church leaflets, the incumbent, local antiquarian societies and the local reference library will be helpful. It is impossible to trace every coat of arms, particularly those assumed improperly in Victorian times.

Women may display badges but are not entitled to display their arms on a shield nor are they permitted a helm or crest. They may display their arms on a lozenge or cartouche. The personal arms of a bishop are impaled with the arms of his See; a rule which also applies to certain office holders.

Achievement	the complete armorial device, including shield, helm, crest, mantling, wreath, supporters, motto, etc. Usually referred to as **armorials** on plate (see p.118).
Badge	device denoting membership of a community, or strictly personal addition to coat of arms; borne by soldiers and servants of the medieval household
Base	bottom of shield
Chief	top of shield
Coat of Arms	displayed on the shield, lozenge or banner
Crest	device borne on the top of the helm
Crest coronet	may replace crest wreath
Crest wreath or torse	wreath hiding joint between crest and helm
Dexter	left side as viewed from the front
Field	ground of shield
Hatchment	the armorial bearings of a deceased person, usually painted on canvas stretched across a lozenge-shaped frame, heavily painted to withstand the weather
Helm	helmet above shield, different according to rank
Impaled	arrangement of two coats of arms side by side on one shield
Insignia	distinguishing mark of an office or honour
Mantling or lambrequin	a short mantle fixed to and flowing from the top of the helm
Shield	central heraldic device bearing arms; varied in shape but variance of no significance
Sinister	right side as viewed from the front

HERALDRY
Terms

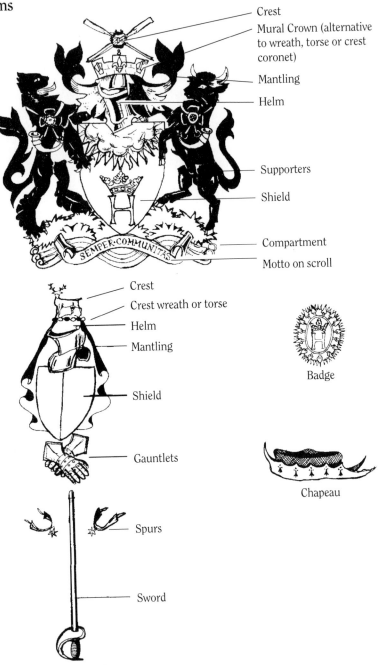

Crest

Mural Crown (alternative to wreath, torse or crest coronet)

Mantling

Helm

Supporters

Shield

Compartment

Motto on scroll

SEMPER·COMMUNITAS

Crest

Crest wreath or torse

Helm

Mantling

Shield

Gauntlets

Spurs

Sword

Badge

Chapeau

Armorial accessories
as displayed in churches

SHIELD SHAPES

Kite   Triangular   À   Spade
        or heater   bouche

POINTS OF THE SHIELD

Chief

Dexter   Sinister

Base

QUARTERINGS

The numbering and
precedence of a simple
quartered shield

*Record the total number of
quarterings together with
the blazon or tricking
of each quarter*

Per pale Or and Gu.
three roundels
counterchanged

DIVISIONS OF THE FIELD

Per fess

Per pale

Per bend

Per bend
sinister

Per chevron

Per pall

Per saltire

Quarterly

HERALDRY
The Shield

VARIED FIELDS

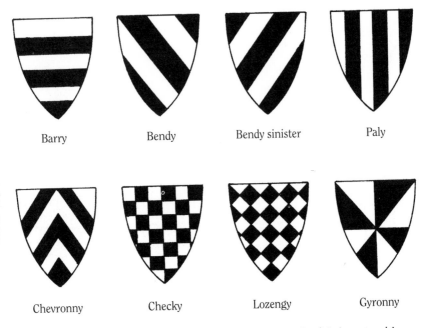

Barry	Bendy	Bendy sinister	Paly
Chevronny	Checky	Lozengy	Gyronny

The field may be varied by division with geometric lines e.g. paly of six Argent and Azure, describes six vertical stripes alternately silver and blue. The lines may be plain or decorated.

If tinctures of the field or charges are reversed on either side of a line of partition, they are said to be counterchanged. (see page 67)

Escutcheon of pretence,
indicates marriage to an heraldic heiress.

The distinguishing mark for baronets (except of Nova Scotia). A white shield charged with a sinister open hand couped at the wrist, Gules.

VARIED LINES

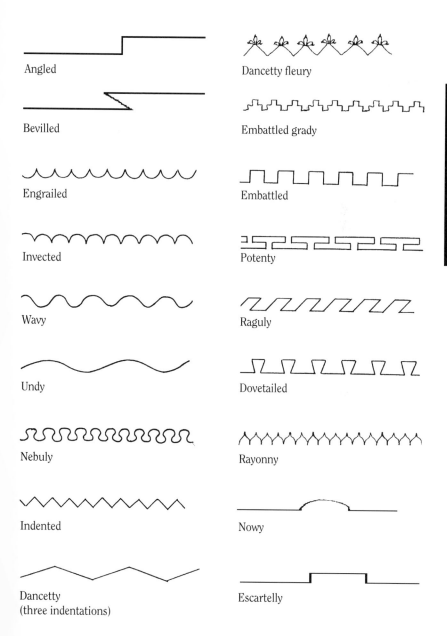

Angled

Bevilled

Engrailed

Invected

Wavy

Undy

Nebuly

Indented

Dancetty
(three indentations)

Dancetty fleury

Embattled grady

Embattled

Potenty

Raguly

Dovetailed

Rayonny

Nowy

Escartelly

HERALDRY
The Shield

TINCTURES & HATCHINGS

There is an exact terminology for armorial tinctures which will be indicated in records by the following hatchings. As a general rule a device of a colour should not be placed on a field of a colour, nor a metal on metal, nor fur on fur. However there are exceptions to this rule.

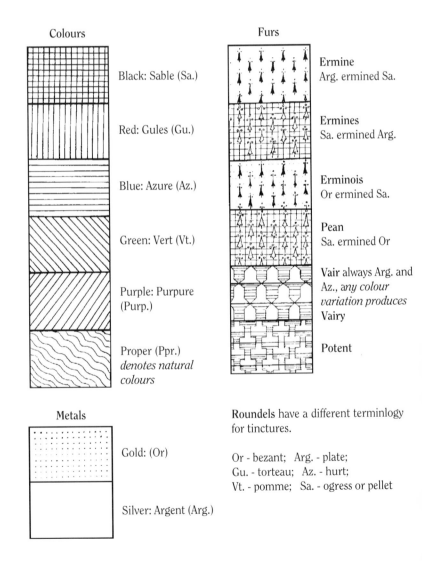

Colours

Black: Sable (Sa.)

Red: Gules (Gu.)

Blue: Azure (Az.)

Green: Vert (Vt.)

Purple: Purpure (Purp.)

Proper (Ppr.) *denotes natural colours*

Metals

Gold: (Or)

Silver: Argent (Arg.)

Furs

Ermine
Arg. ermined Sa.

Ermines
Sa. ermined Arg.

Erminois
Or ermined Sa.

Pean
Sa. ermined Or

Vair always Arg. and Az., *any colour variation produces* Vairy

Potent

Roundels have a different terminlogy for tinctures.

Or - bezant; Arg. - plate;
Gu. - torteau; Az. - hurt;
Vt. - pomme; Sa. - ogress or pellet

CHARGES AND ORDINARIES

A **charge** is any object or figure placed on a shield. Charges may be geometrical (the **Ordinaries** and **Sub-ordinaries**) or any other device, animate or inanimate.

Chief	Fess	Bars	Bars gemels	Fess cotised
Pale	Pallets	Pale endorsed	Bend	Bendlets
Mascle	Bend sinister	Baton	Chevron	Chevronels
Fret	Pile	Piles	Pall	Shakefork
Bordure	Escutcheon	Orle	Double tressure	Canton
Billet	Flaunches	Label	Lozenge	Fusil

HERALDRY
The Shield

ATTITUDES
The attitudes of living creatures should be described. The terminology of attitudes for lions is shown below. Terminology varies for other animals.

Rampant

Rampant
guardant

Rampant
reguardant

Salient

Statant
guardant

Passant

Sejant

Couchant

Dormant

Lions
addorsed

Lions
combatant

Lion rampant
double-headed

CADENCY MARKS
Denote seniority in a family and sometimes distinguish one branch from another.

Eldest son
Label

2nd son
Crescent

3rd son
Mullet

4th son
Martlet

5th son
Annulet

6th son
Fleur-de-
Lys

7th son
Rose

8th son
Cross
Moline

9th son
Double
quatrefoil

72

HELMS

King and royal family
gold, six bars affrontée

Baronet or knight
steel, vizor raised,
affrontée

Earl, peer or baron
silver, garnished with
gold four or five bars,
(shown facing the
dexter)

Gentleman or esquire
steel, vizor closed,
(shown facing the
dexter)

CROWNS & CORONETS

Between the helm and the crest is either a **wreath** or a **cap of maintenance** (or **chapeau**) or a **crest coronet**. (See p.66) This may be a **ducal coronet** of fleurs-de-lys (nothing to do with dukes), a **naval** or a **mural crown**.

Crowns which appear elsewhere, apart from Crowns of Rank, include the **Eastern** and the **Celestial crown**.

Naval Crown

Eastern Crown

Ducal Crown

Celestial Crown

HERALDRY
Crowns and Coronets of Rank

Duke's coronet
Eight strawberry leaves of equal height, five visible

Marquess's coronet
Four strawberry leaves alternating with four pearls of equal height, three leaves and two pearls visible

Earl's coronet
Eight pearls on long points alternating with eight short strawberry leaves, five pearls and four leaves visible

Viscount's coronet
Sixteen pearls on rim, eight or nine pearls visible

Baron's coronet
Six pearls on rim, four visible

Royal crown
(worn by King and King's heir). Four crosses patée alternating with fleurs-de-lys

King's crown has diadems springing from the crosses and the junction is surmounted by a mount bearing another cross patée

Heir's crown is similar but with only two diadems

Royal coronet worn by younger sons and brothers of kings similar to royal crown but without diadems and cross, surmounted by golden tassel

74

The heraldry of hatchments is not always accurate and the motto not always that of the family; silver and gold are indicated by white and yellow. The dexter side is the male side, except for bishops and others holding certain public office. The background is always black behind the arms of the deceased. Variations occur when the arms of more than one wife are depicted.

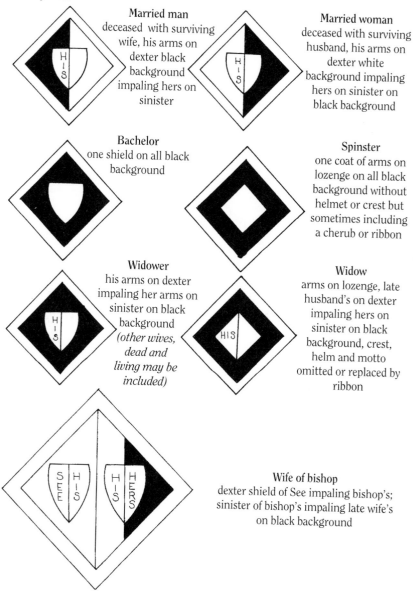

Married man
deceased with surviving wife, his arms on dexter black background impaling hers on sinister

Married woman
deceased with surviving husband, his arms on dexter white background impaling hers on sinister on black background

Bachelor
one shield on all black background

Spinster
one coat of arms on lozenge on all black background without helmet or crest but sometimes including a cherub or ribbon

Widower
his arms on dexter impaling her arms on sinister on black background *(other wives, dead and living may be included)*

Widow
arms on lozenge, late husband's on dexter impaling hers on sinister on black background, crest, helm and motto omitted or replaced by ribbon

Wife of bishop
dexter shield of See impaling bishop's; sinister of bishop's impaling late wife's on black background

Skull in place of crest is said to indicate the extinction of a family

HERALDRY
Hatchments

BLAZONING
Hatchment of Donald Cameron of Lochiel d. 1858

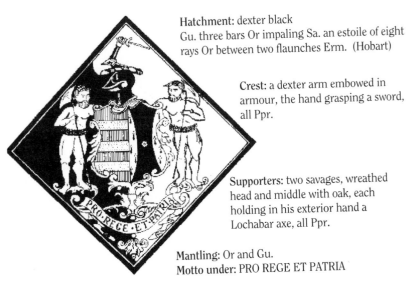

Hatchment: dexter black
Gu. three bars Or impaling Sa. an estoile of eight rays Or between two flaunches Erm. (Hobart)

Crest: a dexter arm embowed in armour, the hand grasping a sword, all Ppr.

Supporters: two savages, wreathed head and middle with oak, each holding in his exterior hand a Lochabar axe, all Ppr.

Mantling: Or and Gu.
Motto under: PRO REGE ET PATRIA

TRICKING
Hatchment of Donald Cameron of Lochiel d. 1858

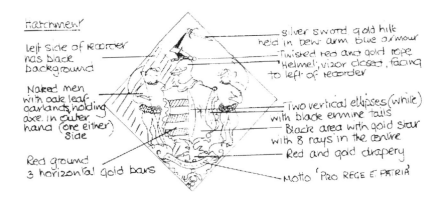

Hatchment

Left side of recorder has black background

Naked men with oak leaf garlands, holding axe in outer hand (one either) side

Red ground 3 horizontal gold bars

silver sword, gold hilt held in Dext arm blue armour
Twisted red and gold rope
Helmet, vizor closed, facing to left of recorder
Two vertical ellipses (white) with black ermine tails
Black area with gold star with 8 rays in the centre
Red and gold drapery
Motto 'PRO REGE ET PATRIA'

pre 1340
Gules, three lions passant guardant in pale Or

1340-1405
1 & 4 France
2 & 3 England

1405-1603
1 & 4 France modern
2 & 3 England

1603-1707
1 & 4 quarterly France and England
2 Scotland
   (Or, a lion rampant within a double tressure flory counterflory Gu.)
3 Ireland
   (Az. a harp Or, stringed Arg.)

1689-1702
1 & 4 quarterly France and England
2 Scotland
3 Ireland Escutcheon: arms of Nassau
   (Az. billety charged with a lion rampant Or)

1707-1714
1 & 4 England impaling Scotland
2 France modern
3 Ireland

1714-1801
1 England impaling Scotland
2 France modern
3 Ireland
4 Hanover

1801-1816
1 & 4 England
2 Scotland
3 Ireland
Escutcheon: arms of Hanover ensigned with electoral cap

1816-37
1 & 4 England
2 Scotland
3 Ireland
Escutcheon: arms of Hanover ensigned with crown

HERALDRY
Royal Arms

1837 onwards

Arms
quarterly, 1st and 4th (England), Gu. three lions pass. guard. in pale Or; 2nd (Scotland) Or, a lion ramp. within a double tressure flory counterflory Gu.; 3rd (Ireland) Az. a harp Or, stringed Arg; the whole encircled with the Garter

Crest	Upon the royal helmet, the imperial crown Ppr, thereon a lion statant guardant Or, imperially crowned Ppr.
Supporters	Dexter, a lion ramp. guard., Or, crowned as the crest; sinister, an unicorn Arg. armed, crined and unguled Or, gorged with a coronet composed of crosses patée and fleurs-de-lys, a chain affixed thereto, passing between the fore-legs and reflexed over the back Or
Motto	*DIEU ET MON DROIT* in the compartment below the shield; with the Union rose, shamrock and thistle engrafted on the same stem
Crown of England	a circle Or, issuing therefrom 4 crosses patée and 4 fleurs-de-lys, arranged alternately; from the crosses patée arise two arched diadems Or ornamented with pearls, closing at the top under a mound, surmounted by a cross patée also Or, the whole enriched with precious stones; cap of crimson velvet turned up Erm.

Badges

England	red and white rose united
Scotland	thistle
Ireland	a harp Or, stringed Arg. shamrock leaf Vert
Wales	dragon pass. wings elevated Gu. upon a mound Vert

All ensigned with the royal crown.

A standard description "Royal Arms as used from 1837" can be used to replace full blazoning.

78

ORDERS OF KNIGHTHOOD

The symbols of orders will appear on the insignia and the arms will include the motto.

The Order of the Garter	with buckle
	"Honi soit qui mal y pense"
The Order of the Thistle	saltire cross and thistle
	"Nemo me impune lacessit"
The Order of St Patrick	shamrock
	"Quis separabit"
The Order of the Bath	Maltese cross with rose, thistle and shamrock in centre
	"Tria juncta in uno"
The Star of India	*"Heaven's light our guide"*
The Order of St Michael and St George	*"Auspicium Melioris Aevi"*
The Order of Victoria and Albert	Queen Victoria and Prince Albert in profile

ECCLESIASTICAL ARMS

Each See has its own arms. The chief provinces of the Church of England are the Archiepiscopal Sees of Canterbury and York. There is no helm or crest with personal arms of the clergy.

Canterbury
Az. an archiepiscopal cross in pale Or surmounted by a pall Ppr. charged with four crosses patée fitchée Sa.

York
Gu. two keys in saltire Arg. in chief a regal crown

LETTERING
Terms

Lettering appears on memorials, in books and manuscripts, on stained and engraved glass and textiles. It is possible to consider a general approach to the classification of lettering but in addition, specific systems exist for the identification of silver, pewter and ceramics.

Applied   individual letters cast or carved and pinned to the surface of buildings and memorials; commonly of gilded wood, brass, bronze and lead

Flat   painted or gilded directly onto the surface; a fine outline may show around letters painted on stone

Incised   cut into the surface. Letters may be painted in a colour or filled with lead or mastic.

| V-Cut | Gouged | Lowered | Cushioned |

Raised   background cut away leaving letters in relief; may be raised, domed or raised with inline

| Raised | Domed | Raised with inline |

On manuscripts and in calligraphy, the capital and small letters are described as **majuscules** and **minuscules** respectively. However, printing has provided the widest terminology for describing letterforms. The terms **upper case** and **lower case** derive from the type cases of printers where the case of capital letters lies above that of small letters. Today, **capital letters** and **lower case** letters are the terms most generally understood WHEN DESCRIBING ALL LETTERING OTHER THAN MANUSCRIPTS.

Cap. line
x height   N K G n k g   Ascender

Base line   Descender
Drop line   Serifs

ABDEKMRX

| Light | Medium | Bold | Extra Bold |

Weight   described as light; medium; **bold** or **extra bold**

DISPLAYWORK STAR

| Condensed | Expanded |

Width   described as condensed or expanded
Latin Condensed type or *Latin Expanded type*

REPRO *ADM*

Decorated · · Flourished ·

Decorated letters	elaborations of a basic form *Fry's Ornamented type*
Flourished	part of the basic letter, either roman or italic extended into a flourished shape. *Perpetua type, italic capitals*

ABCD ABCab

· Outlined · Shaded ·

Outlined/shaded	outlined or shaded to give the impression of a third dimension. *Grotesque Outline type or Chisel Shaded type*

MP·CAES

Classical roman	the word **roman** has several meanings and it is important to distinguish between them. During the 1st century AD inscriptional lettering in Rome had its greatest flowering. The Trajan inscription is one fine example. The style of lettering which it portrays is referred to as Classical roman.

ABCEMORS
abcdefghimop

Roman	printing term denoting both capital and lower case letters which are upright as opposed to sloped or italic and which have their roots in the Classical roman letters. *Perpetua type, designed by Eric Gill*

ABCEMORST
abcdefghimnop

Italic
sloped version of roman. The name stems from the letterforms of Italian writing masters of the 16th century which in fact hardly sloped at all.

Sloped roman
term used by letter designers, but italic is generally understood to refer to that style of letter which leans to the right.
Perpetua italic type

ABC abcd ⌐

Sans serif
letterforms characterised by a lack of serifs and a more even width of stroke throughout each letter. Within this group are types variously described as **Grotesque**, **Glyptic** and, confusingly, **Gothic** but sans serif is the simplest and most commonly used description.

ABCabcd ⌐

Clarendon
letters with bracketed serifs, derived from the typeface of that name. It is found incised on many 18th and 19th century gravestones.

ABC abcd ⌐

Egyptian
letters with square serifs, used extensively on memorials in various weights and sets.
Rockwell type

ABCDEF
abcdefgh

Latin
letters with triangular serifs.
Latin Expanded type

LETTERING

𝕬 𝕭 𝕮 𝖆𝖇𝖈

Gothic   letters with strong vertical pen stress, evenly spaced elements and angular terminals with wide variations showing condensation, expansion, decoration and flourishing. Also known as **Black Letter** in medieval manuscripts.
Old English type

Effect may be copied

Copper plate   well known 18th century pen style.
Marina Script type

MANUSCRIPT LETTERFORMS

Of the great variety of manuscript styles developed in Europe from the 1st century AD, these examples represent clear stages in the development of writing.

RATESETMYSTICAVANN
AFAIVLIOANIEMEMORI

Majuscules   or *Square capitals* from a 3rd century Virgil in the Vatican Library,
Quadrata   Cod. Vat. 3256

TESTATVAMORITVRADEOS
SIDERATVMSIQVODNONA

Rustica   or *Rustic capitals* from a 4th century Virgil in the Vatican Library,
Cod. Palat. Lat. 1631

fecerunt oculi,

Uncials   from 5th century manuscript in the British Library, Cotton MS Vespasian A.i.

abate bibere

Half uncials   from 7th century Lindisfarne Gospels, British Library, Cotton MS Nero D.iv.

LETTERING
Styles

R A L O M

Versals   based on a 7th century manuscript

hunc ab ordio mo

Roman Script   script based on 9th century Carolingian pen writing, Bodelian MS, E.D. Clarke 28

aboram clamant

Gothic   Gothic book hand from 13th century York Psalter, British Library 54179

delectatio afferretur

Italic   Early 16th century italic script Arrighi *(attributed)*, British Library, Royal MS 12C VIII.

84

TWO-DIMENSIONAL SHAPES

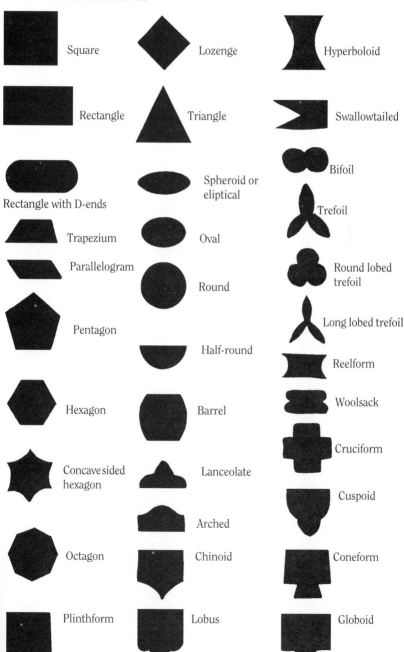

Square

Lozenge

Hyperboloid

Rectangle

Triangle

Swallowtailed

Rectangle with D-ends

Spheroid or eliptical

Bifoil

Trapezium

Oval

Trefoil

Parallelogram

Round

Round lobed trefoil

Pentagon

Half-round

Long lobed trefoil

Hexagon

Barrel

Reelform

Concave sided hexagon

Lanceolate

Woolsack

Octagon

Arched

Cruciform

Chinoid

Cuspoid

Plinthform

Lobus

Coneform

Globoid

SHAPES AND MOULDINGS
Universal Shapes

THREE-DIMENSIONAL SHAPES

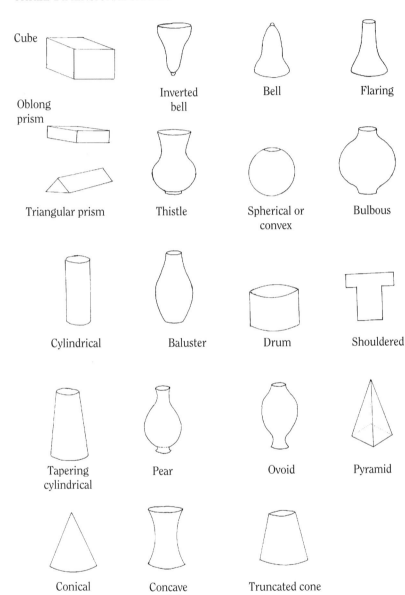

Cube

Oblong
prism

Triangular prism

Inverted
bell

Thistle

Bell

Spherical or
convex

Flaring

Bulbous

Cylindrical

Tapering
cylindrical

Conical

Baluster

Pear

Concave
sided

Drum

Ovoid

Truncated cone

Shouldered

Pyramid

COMPLEX SHAPES

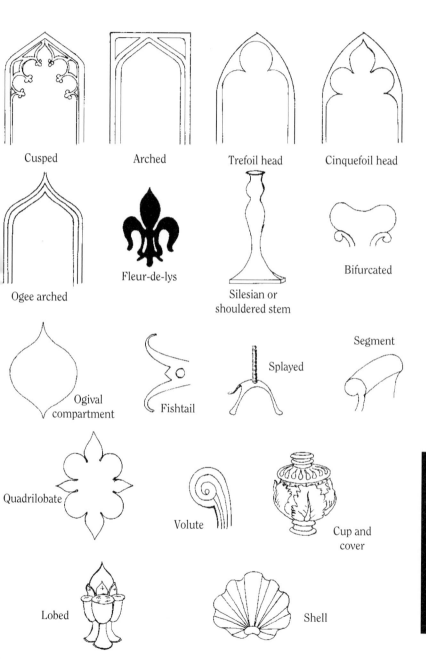

Cusped

Arched

Trefoil head

Cinquefoil head

Ogee arched

Fleur-de-lys

Silesian or
shouldered stem

Bifurcated

Ogival
compartment

Fishtail

Splayed

Segment

Quadrilobate

Volute

Cup and
cover

Lobed

Shell

SHAPES & MOULDINGS
Cups, Plates and Jugs

Baluster
(or pear or tulip)

Baluster

Squat baluster
(Pewter vessels: Bulbous or bellied)

Bombe

Lip

Cylindrical

Tapering
cylindrical
(Pewter vessels: Truncated cone)

Tall
cylindrical

Skirt

Tall tapering
cylindrical with
skirt

Barrel

Barrel

Boat

Drum

Helmet

Urn
(or vase or
ovoid)

Hexagonal
stepped stand or
socle

Plate-shaped

Dish-shaped or
basin-shaped

Bowl-shaped or
saucer-shaped

Cup-shaped

Flat

Pomegranate

Ball

Ring

Raised flat-topped

Bud

Cross

Flame

Bun

Lobed

Crown

Bell

Cap

Dove

Banded Knop

Urn

Beefeater

Lobed and foliated

Acorn

Baluster

High domed

Orb

Cone

Ball and Steeple

Domed

Stepped domed

Double domed

Waisted

SHAPES & MOULDINGS

89

SHAPES & MOULDINGS
Feet and Handles

Arcaded

High
circular

Tuck-in base on
spreading rim

Stud

Incurving

Trumpet

Bun

Standard
or loop

Lobed
quatrefoil

Circular moulded
spreading

Ball

Angular

Shaped lobed
or wavy

Domed on
narrow flange

Reeded base

Baluster

Paw

Spreading
skirt

Hexagonal
spreading moulded

Capped scroll

Cusped tripod

Shallow dome or
spreading conical

Shell and
scroll

Scroll

Stepped circular

High conical

Flying scroll

Broken or double
scroll

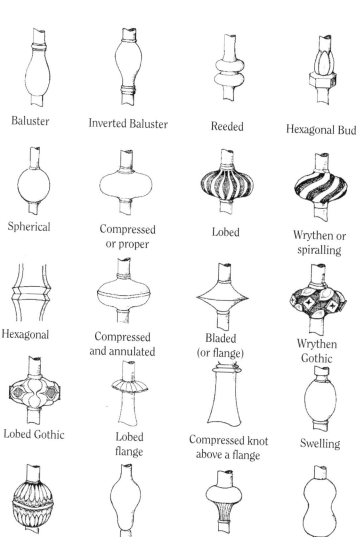

Baluster   Inverted Baluster   Reeded   Hexagonal Bud

Spherical   Compressed   Lobed   Wrythen or
or proper   spiralling

Hexagonal   Compressed   Bladed   Wrythen
             and annulated   (or flange)   Gothic

Lobed Gothic   Lobed   Compressed knot   Swelling
             flange   above a flange

Cup and cover   Shouldered   Mushroom   Dumb-bell
or melon

Cushioned   Cone   Acorn   Multi-knotted

SHAPES & MOULDINGS

SHAPES & MOULDINGS
Mouldings

Mouldings are plain or enriched projecting or recessed bands of decoration either worked directly (**struck**) or **applied**.

Bead and butt	moulding worked on 2 sides of panel
Bead and flush	moulding worked on all 4 sides of panel
Pulvinated	with cushion-like swelling
Quirk	groove running parallel to bead

The names of mouldings follow classical rules for all styles except gothic mouldings which have their own terminology, here represented in brackets where the moulding style exists.

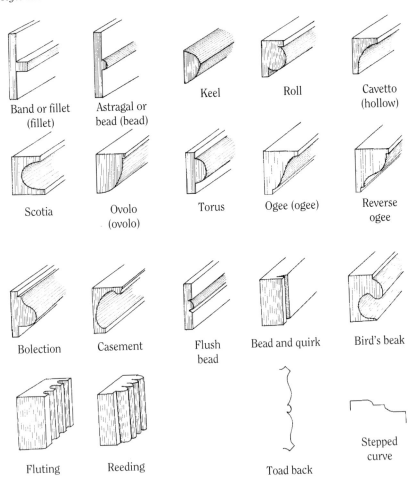

Band or fillet (fillet)

Astragal or bead (bead)

Keel

Roll

Cavetto (hollow)

Scotia

Ovolo (ovolo)

Torus

Ogee (ogee)

Reverse ogee

Bolection

Casement

Flush bead

Bead and quirk

Bird's beak

Fluting

Reeding

Toad back

Stepped curve

MATERIALS

CERAMICS
Marks

Ceramics include objects made of porcelain and pottery. Ceramics other than tiles are not common in churches but are occasionally encountered, possibly an early pottery jug or a china vase. Even a cracked 18th century piece may be of value. If you do find a ceramic piece you will probably need a detailed reference book. *See FURTHER READING.*

PORCELAIN   is *translucent* unless the body is very thick. The body is white and almost invariably has a transparent glaze, which may be slightly blued. Vases etc. are glazed inside and out.

POTTERY   is *opaque*, the clay body varying from brown, grey, red, orange to white. When the body is not white, a white opaque glaze may be used to imitate porcelain. The clay body is porous so has to be glazed, at least on the inside, if it is to hold liquid.

MARKS

Many ceramic pieces are marked, usually on the base, with the factory mark and/or the decorator's or potter's marks. These marks are found both under the glaze and over the glaze and may be painted, printed, incised or impressed. Since in the 18th and 19th centuries many factories copied the marks of other factories, marks alone are unreliable for attribution purposes.

Make a note of the mark, if there is one, and consult your local museum or someone knowledgeable on ceramics if you think the piece is of interest.

Between 1842 and 1883 a registration mark was used by many manufacturers in the UK which gave copyright protection.

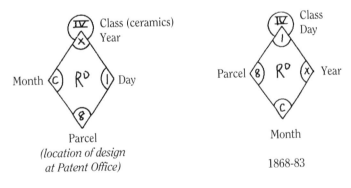

Class (ceramics)
Year
Month
Day
Parcel
(location of design at Patent Office)

1842-67

Class
Day
Parcel
Year
Month

1868-83

A simple registration number only was used from 1884-1901.

An item marked *'England'* dates from 1891 or later, an item marked *'Made in England'* dates from the 20th century.

Here are a few marks commonly found on ceramics in English houses which may have found their way into churches.

Meissen but copied and adapted by numerous factories.

Bow, Chelsea, Derby, Venice, or 19th century copies all used an anchor mark but the shape may vary.

Derby c. 1785-1830 similar marks in red, blue or purple, or incised

18th century English soft paste.

typical fancy outline used by Victorian factories, usually incorporating the pattern name and number

Wedgwood
note the full mark, lettering and spelling, as other firms using the name, often spelt Wedgewood, would not be genuine.

18th century **Sparrow Beak** jug, small with ribbed, smooth or patterned surfaces.

Mid 19th century **Dragon Vase** with six-character mark of *K'ang Hsi* dynasty. Globular body and cylindrical neck, decorated with nine scaly five-clawed dragons, all of different colour and with ferocious expressions, on a ground of white crested waves painted in underglaze blue.

Record the mark accurately and in detail with a photograph or drawing and a note of the shape, glaze, colour and design. Recognise the difference between underglaze and decoration over the glaze. Record even unmarked underglaze items. Anything handpainted, unless obviously of amateur workmanship, is of interest.

CERAMICS
Floor Tiles

MEDIEVAL FLOOR TILES

Plain Tiles
Plain lead glazed earthenware tiles were probably introduced in the 12th century and were made in various sizes. Glazed with a lead glaze applied direct to the body or over white-slip or with added copper, the tiles were brown, yellow, or green to black. Yellow and green/black tiles were often laid chequerwise. Such hand-made plain glazed tiles are still in use.

Mosaic Tiles
Plain glazed mosaic may have been introduced as early as 1180 but most was made during the 13th century. Most arrangements were formed with rectilinear shapes but more intricate arrangements, including elaborate shapes, were used in important parts of the church. Yellow and green/black tiles were used alternately. Decoration was added to some elements of the mosaic arrangements from the 1230s, relief, linear or two-colour motifs being employed. All decorative designs were applied to the surface of the tile with a carved wooden stamp when the unfired tile was leather hard. The making of all mosaics was labour intensive and they were never mass-produced, few being made after the 1340s.

Relief Tiles
Relief decoration, either upstanding or depressed, was introduced in the late 12th century and continued in use until the 16th century and until the 18th century in Devon. Each tile was glazed a single colour, brown, yellow, green or black. Pavements were sometimes laid in alternating colours, sometimes in one colour only.

Line-impressed Tiles
During the early 14th century to the 16th century linear decoration was stamped on monochrome tiles. These also were laid either in alternating colours or in one colour only.

Two-colour Tiles
These tiles were introduced in the 1230s at first for special commissions but by the 1260s were also mass-produced. They became the most popular type and were made until the mid-16th century. As with the monochrome tiles the design was stamped on the surface of the leather hard tile with a wooden stamp on which the design was upstanding. The cavities so formed were filled with white firing clay introduced in various ways. On the earlier 'inlaid' tiles the white clay was pressed in a plastic state and in the later 15th and the 16th centuries it was often poured in as liquid slip. Other methods, less easily recognised, were also used. Both specially commissioned and mass-produced two-colour tiles were made throughout the period except for a few decades after the Black Death when few if any special tiles were commissioned.

The best documented tilery was operating at Penn in Buckinghamshire from the 1330s to the 1380s. During this period its tiles were widely distributed in neighbouring counties and as far away as Kent and Surrey. There were certainly many more such tileries for which no records survive. The two-colour tiles were those most commonly reproduced during the Gothic revival.

Fleur-de-lys between four quadrants, each enclosing an embattled quadrant and a quarter octofoil. (Penn)

Design based on the Solomon's Seal with a quatrefoil at the centre within a star. (Penn)

Part of a four-tile design of formal foliage in a quatrefoil, with foliage and fleurs-de-lys cut out by a quadrant in the outer angles. Surface damaged in two places. (Wessex)

A repeating 4-tile design of cinquefoils within circles powdered with lozenges, set in a square with foliated motifs in the spandrels and centre, alternating with squares enclosing conjoined fleurs-de-lys. (Wessex)

97

CERAMICS
Floor Tiles

VICTORIAN FLOOR TILES

Quarry Tiles

Although this term is often applied to a wide range of plain floor tiles it is correctly used only for tiles which are moulded, cut or extruded from plastic (or wet) clay and unglazed. These tiles were much used in Victorian times for the aisles of churches and were usually laid in chequer patterns using red and black or red and buff tiles. The most common size is 15cm square but 10cm and 22.5cm were also used. Mainly produced in the Potteries and Wales, these tiles often have a coarse surface which contrasts with the smooth flat surface of dustpressed tiles.

Dustpressed Tiles

In 1840, Richard Prosser of Birmingham patented a method of producing ceramic buttons by drying clay to a fine dust which was then put in a powerful press, thus forming the button rapidly and accurately. Herbert Minton bought a share in the patent and realized that the process could be applied to the manufacture of tiles and by 1842 was producing smooth flat floor tiles in several colours. Because they were easier to clean than quarry tiles they soon became very popular and were used in the same way as quarry tiles or to form surrounds for encaustic tiles *(see below)*. As well as squares, many other shapes were made which were usually based on geometric portions of a 15cm square and these were laid utilising the many colours in large mosaic designs known as **Geometric Pavements**.

Encaustic Tiles

Herbert Minton produced reproductions of medieval encaustic tiles for use in Gothic Revival restorations from about 1835. Victorian encaustic tiles are easily recognized as they are usually far more precise and mechanical in design and manufacture than their predecessors. By 1860 many new colours had been introduced, often as many as eight on a single tile. Early tiles are normally unglazed or glazed over the inlay only, using a yellow majolica glaze. Later tiles, from about 1850 onwards, usually have a clear glaze or are fired to a higher (vitreous) temperature which makes them much less porous. Victorian encaustic tiles are quite often marked with the makers' name on the back and sometimes a **trade tile** was included which gives the makers' name and address. Common makers' names are Mintons, Maws, Godwins, Craven Dunnill and Campbells.

Fourfold foliate design in quatrefoil. Block printed in black on white body under clear glaze. Manufactured by MINTON HOLLINS & CO (Minton & Co) c. 1845. Prossers Patent Dustpressed Method. (Marks moulded on reverse).

Sacred Monogram IHS interlaced in stylised quatrefoil with quarter roses at corners. Red, white, yellow, orange, mauve & blue Majolica glazes on dustpressed body. MINTONS & CO c. 1855 (Marks moulded on reverse).

Encaustic tile with design of St. George on horseback based on a medieval original from the Temple Church, London. Design adapted by A.W.N. Pugin for Herbert Minton. c. 1850 (MINTON & CO. impressed on reverse) Unglazed.

Pseudo-medieval encaustic tile with cinquefoil in white and stylized foliate corners. Surface distressed to represent medieval tile. W. GODWIN c. 1865 (Impressed marks on reverse) Worn glaze.

METAL
Terms

There are metal objects all around churches, some are precious, some workaday; some are functional, some merely decorative; some have much in common with ceramics, some with wooden objects, some with stone.

Various aspects of metal objects are of interest, their use, the metal they are made of, the marks, armorials and inscriptions they bear, their size and date. Decoration, particularly in medieval work, often demonstrates the same features and style as contemporary architecture.

TYPES OF METAL

Bell metal	alloy of copper and tin
Brass	alloy of copper and zinc
Britannia metal	hard form of pewter, appears similar to silver or polished pewter, it is produced in sheet form and thus permits cold processing of the metal such as spinning, die-stamping and hand-forming. In use from the 1780's until present day.
Britannia silver	95.8 per cent pure silver
Bronze	alloy of copper, tin and other metal
Electroplate	method of laying fine particles of silver onto base metal, introduced in 1840's
EPBM	electroplated Britannia metal (after 1850). Makers' names and catalogue numbers may be found impressed into metal
EPGS	electroplated German silver (electroplated nickel silver)
EPNS	electroplated nickel silver, from c.1840
Nickel silver	alloy of copper, zinc and nickel, often passed off as silver by mis-describing nickel eg. German silver
Ormolu	gilded bronze or copper alloy, mostly used for mounts
Parcel gilt	silver with part coating of gold
Pewter	greyish alloy of tin with small amounts of lead and/or copper and/or antimony. Bright like silver when new but oxidises with time to grey appearance. Makers' marks often found (see p. 103)
Sheffield Plate	copper sandwiched and fused between layers of sterling silver and rolled into sheets for use, made from 1760-1840. Seams are dovetailed and edges often rolled to disguise the sandwich. Marks, when found, are similar to hallmarks on early pieces, later a manufacturer's name or symbol may be indented
Silver gilt	silver with coating of gold
Silver plate	utensils of silver
Silver plated	articles of metal with thin coating of silver
Sterling standard	92.5 per cent silver

DECORATIVE TECHNIQUES

Annulated	decorated with rings
Applied	ornament or part overlaid onto a surface
Cast	pattern made by running molten metal into a mould
Chasing	metal decorated by means of hammer-blows pushing along a punch to indent a pattern
Embossing or repoussé	metal hammered from the back to form bosses or raised patterns. Often used in conjunction with chasing
Enamelling	enamel is finely ground glass, coloured by metallic oxides, fused by heat to a metal surface. It may be matte or gloss, opaque, translucent or opalescent. The various kinds of enamelling include:-

Basse-taille:	level-topped layer of transparent enamel laid over sculptured and chased metal in low relief, with consequent variation in the depth of colour
Champlevé:	recesses in the metal ground are filled with enamel
Cloisonné:	cells of wire or narrow strips of metal, on a metal ground enclose areas of colour
Dipped:	enamelling in the round, found on sculpture and jewellery
Painted:	a metal foundation, usually slightly domed, enamelled overall on both sides, then brush-decorated, often over a transfer print
Plique-à-jour:	*(light of day)*: pierced metal or cloissons hold transparent enamels so that light passes through like stained-glass
Printed:	transfer or bat-printed, usually monochrome on a plain enamelled ground

Engraving	removal of metal by sharp tools, used particularly for lettering and armorials (early 18th century armorials cast, chased or applied)
Finial	decorative knob on top of lid, cover or upright etc. or terminal at base of handle
Hatched/matted	engraved lines, small circles or dots produced by a hollow punch
Knot	protrusion on stem
Niello	engraved lines or depressions filled with black composition
Swan-necked handle	double curving feature similar to scrolling
Thumbpiece	finial rising from top of handle to be held by the thumb
Reed	ring cast on or near the outside edge of a pewter plate
Wriggle-work	method of decorating or drawing on pewter by rocking the end of a chisel or other tool backwards and forwards to produce zig-zag lines

METAL
Marks

Metal marks generally consist of a **maker's mark**; a **metal mark**; for precious metals, an **Assay Office Mark**; and a **date letter**. A detailed pocket guide to marks is an essential tool. The first mark is the Sponsor's or maker's mark, the second is usually the sterling mark, the third is the Assay Office (and this will vary according to which Assay Office tested the article), and the fourth is the date letter mark, indicating the year of assay, as this is changed annually and varies according to the assay town. The shape of the shields and the type of alphabet are all vital, as are any distinguishing dots, crowns etc. Component parts should carry some marks but only one complete set per item.

Sponsor or   Sterling   Assay Office   Date letter
maker's mark

Sterling silver standard
Leopard's head mark (1300 to present day), crowned leopard's head (1478-1821). Lion passant 1544-1697 and 1720 to present day (92.5 per cent silver) if supported by Assay Office mark.

Britannia silver standard
Figure of Britannia used from 1697 to the present day, replaced sterling compulsorily from 1697-1720, thereafter optional. Britannia mark used in conjunction with the Lion's head erased (torn off at the neck) until 1975, therafter Britannia only. Assay Offices other than London have their town mark in addition. From 1784-1890 an extra, temporary mark was used, which was the **duty mark**, the mark was the monarch's head, so during this period 5 marks will be found on a piece of London silver, and 6 on most Provincial silver.

Gold
Marked in the same way as sterling standard until 18ct was introduced in 1798. Other lower carats were introduced from mid 19th century. The shape of the date letter shield can differ from silver although the letter is the same.

Platinum
Marks were introduced in 1975. Similar marks to gold and silver except that the standard mark is an orb surmounted by a cross within a pentagon.

Commemorative Mark
For the year of the Silver Jubilee (1934-5) of King George V and Queen Mary, the Coronation (1952-3) and Silver Jubilee (1977) of Queen Elizabeth II, an extra optional mark was introduced, showing the sovereign's head.

Foreign plate
From 1842 all imported plate sold had to be submitted for assay and marking. From 1867 to 1904 an extra mark of F in an oval punch was required to be struck. From 1904 distinct import marks were introduced, (a square punch being used for gold, an oval punch for silver), numerical punches were introduced for standards, and the current date letter was also struck.

PEWTER

Touch mark	the primary mark which gives the name of the Pewterer. Of many shapes, styles and designs.
Hallmarks	usually four small punched marks, the use of which brought forth protests from the Goldsmiths, which infer neither date, town or quality but are the choice of an individual pewterer and are an extra means of determining his or her identity. First used about 1635.
Rose and crown	used from at least 1566 as a quality mark on pewter in Britain. It is used on the Continent as a touch mark.
Crowned X	believed to be a quality mark, signifying extraordinary or hard pewter alloy, ie. an alloy containing more antimony than usual.

DECORATION
A great variety of decorative forms appear on metal items.

| 13th & 14th century stamped tendril ornament | 17th & 18th century wrought iron waterleaf | 17th & 18th century repoussé sheet iron acanthus | 18th century cast iron medallion |

Twist

Fish tail

Ribbon end

Ribbon end scroll

Scrolls

Clip collars

Rolled nib

Open scarf collar

Astragal collar

Solid barrel or bolt end

Flat nib or half-penny snub

Fiddlehead

THUMBPIECES

Ramshorn or
Corkscrew

Volute

Scroll

Moulded

Chair

Twin lobe

Open

Pierced

Pomegranate

Bud

Hammerhead

Embryo shell

Bifurcated leaf

Bifurcated

FINIALS OR TERMINALS
at the base of handles

Rat tail

Fish tail

Heel

Spade

Ball

Attention

Shield

Leaf

Scroll

METAL

105

METAL
Fixtures

HINGES

The earliest metal hinges in Norman times recall Viking designs, being usually crescent-shaped with snake-head, tendril or flower terminals. By the 12th century hinges had become more geometrical. The greatest period for metalwork decoration was the 13th century when scrollwork was widely used, before a decline in the quality of blacksmiths' work in the 14th century.

Like handles, hinges are unreliable for dating purposes, since all styles have been copied throughout the centuries.

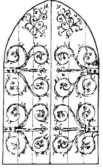

17th century wrought-iron **Strap-hinge** with stamped decoration on the fleur-de-lys finial

Strap-hinge with incised chevron decoration and fleur-de-lys finial

Decorative strap-hinges
Horizontal straps with diverging channelled scrolled stems and leaves

Gudgeon-hook smithed to a wrought iron lug, over which the eye of the strap-hinge sometimes passed

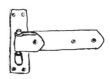

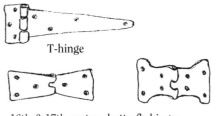

T-hinge

Pin hung **hook-and-band hinge**, the eye (formed by the band return) passing over a pin

16th & 17th century **butterfly hinges**

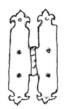

16th & 17th century
Cock's head hinge

18th century **H-hinge** or 20th century **Parliament hinge**

Butt hinge in use from c. 1680

KEYS AND LOCKS

Keys made before 1850 usually have bits filed on the front; after 1850 they are filed on the bottom edge

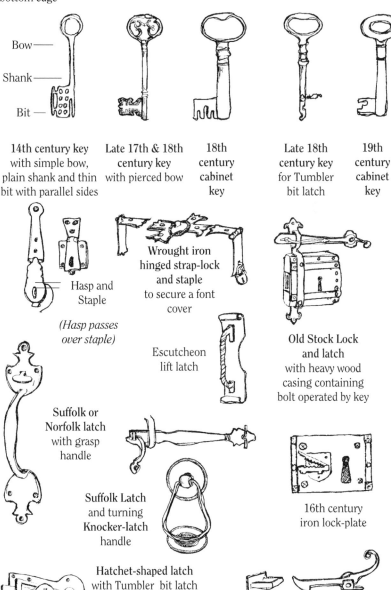

Bow

Shank

Bit

14th century key with simple bow, plain shank and thin bit with parallel sides

Late 17th & 18th century key with pierced bow

18th century cabinet key

Late 18th century key for Tumbler bit latch

19th century cabinet key

Hasp and Staple

(Hasp passes over staple)

Wrought iron hinged strap-lock and staple to secure a font cover

Escutcheon lift latch

Old Stock Lock and latch with heavy wood casing containing bolt operated by key

Suffolk or Norfolk latch with grasp handle

Suffolk Latch and turning Knocker-latch handle

16th century iron lock-plate

Hatchet-shaped latch with Tumbler bit latch lock

Keep *(slot into which a bolt is shot)*

Holdback catch for gates

METAL
Fixtures

HANDLES AND KEY ESCUTCHEONS

Although some handle shapes are typical of a particular period, all have been much copied at different times. Keyholes on English furniture are generally rounded at the base until the 18th century.

1. Square iron lock-plate with trefoil corners 14th, 15th and 16th centuries
2. Iron stirrup with cruciform backplate 16th and 17th centuries
3. Iron loop-drop twist with round backplate 16th and 17th centuries
4. Iron heart-shaped loop-drop on a shaped key escutcheon 16th and 17th centuries
5. Iron ring or Dutch drop (1690-1710)
6. Cast brass pear-drop on circular moulded backplate c.1700
7. Split tail or axe-drop on hexafoil backplate early 18th century
8. Acorn drop c.1700
9. Tangs and loop on engraved and shaped backplate early 18th century
10. Shield-shaped key escutcheon, often engraved, early 18th century
11. Bail handle passing through cast knobs on solid backplate c.1710
12. Bail handle passing through cast knobs on cutaway backplate c.1730
13. Bail handle passing through cast knobs on pierced backplate c.1750
14. 1740-70
15. Dutch drop from 1750
16. Swan-necked loop from 2 circular moulded backplates from 1750 and much used in the 19th century
17. Mid 18th century Chinoiserie with geometric piercing
18. Rococo with 2 separate plates for handle sockets and acanthus decoration (decoration sometimes asymmetrical) from c.1750. Earlier examples have a single backplate
19. From 1770
20. Relief-stamped oval backplate with plain loop handle passing through two knobs from c.1770
21. Circular relief-stamped handle on circular moulded backplate from c. 1770
22. Lion mask with ring 1790-1820
23. Relief-stamped swan-necked handle attached to oval rose-stamped backplates
24. Beaded circular loop attached to stamped circular backplate c. 1820
25. Sunken or recessed handle often found on military or travelling chests c.1820
26. Art nouveau fixed protruding loop c.1900

NAILS AND SCREWS

Tapering metal screws were first introduced in the late 17th century and were hand-filed with irregular threads. Lathe-turned screws appeared in the late 18th century and machine-made screws in the mid-19th century.

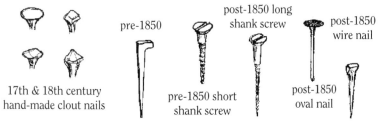

pre-1850

post-1850 long shank screw

post-1850 wire nail

17th & 18th century hand-made clout nails

pre-1850 short shank screw

post-1850 oval nail

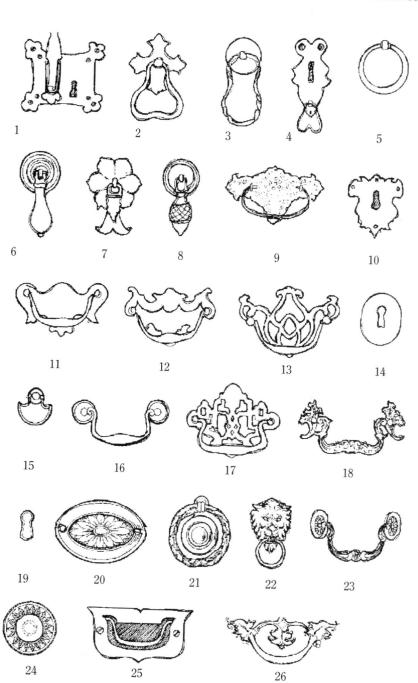

1

2

3

4

5

6

7

8

9

10

11

12

13

14

15

16

17

18

19

20

21

22

23

24

25

26

METAL

METAL
Religious Objects
BAPTISM, HOLY WATER, OIL AND INCENSE

Portable font
Cercelée cross iron finial on lid.
Oak body with metal lift-out bowl.
Hand -forged wrought iron cruciform stand
on oak plinth with chamfered edges

Silver stoup or Holy Water basin
*(usually near the entrance to the church and
more often of stone)*
Backplate of lozenge-shaped cartouche form
with strapwork, repoussé and hammered
decoration, with Sacred Monogram IHS in plain
roman capitals superimposed on a Latin cross
on a central medallion.
Waterleaf decorated bombe basin stepped at
base.
Pendant ball and steeple finial.

Silver asperges bucket
Tubular lobed bail or swing handle.
Moulded floriated double-curved rim.
Vase shaped body with chased decoration of a
cupid head and festoons.
Collet *(collar)* at junction of body and foot.
High domed foot with turned over edge and
matted and scrolled decoration.

Asperges or holy water sprinkler
with perforated ball finial and baluster stem of silver, attached to oak handle with silver baluster knop.

Aspergillum
brush with short handle

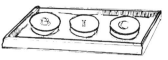

Chrismatory
containing set of Holy Oil Stocks

Baptismal shell
with shaped silver handle on which is an engraved Maltese cross.

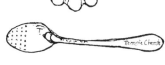

Stem-struck strainer spoon
of Old English pattern c.1730 with elliptical bowl and name of church engraved in script on handle.

Incense dish of boat shape c. 1742
edged with roll moulding, on baluster stem above high circular foot stepped at base.
Double lid, hinged amidship, with ends of flaps secured by cast scrolled clasps projecting from bulwarks.

Censer
Finial encased in a cresting of loops, through which run 3 chains rising from attachments on the base.
Domed and stepped cover with lobed rim, decorated with double roll mouldings, the dome with pierced dormers.
Lobed hexagonal body with everted edge
A roundel applied to each lobe, cusped inside with a spoke pattern ending in trefoils.
Hexagonal foot with double roll edge, each facet being pierced with a hole for attachments, now missing.
Thumbpiece attached to a trefoil plate.

METAL
Religious Objects
BELLS
Bells are hung in the **Bell Chamber**, usually high in the tower or spire of the church. The bells are rung from the **Ringing Chamber** and between them is a **Dead Chamber** or (if it contains a clock) the **Clock Chamber**. In the late 19th century, the Revd. Ellacombe introduced a pulley system for bell chimes which is often found and is known as the **Ellacombe Chiming System**.

Bells frequently have names, the majority feminine, but some male, like Great Tom of Oxford or Big Ben. They are stamped with foundry marks and may carry other inscriptions. The character of the lettering and the foundry marks upon old bells are valuable in determining date, although the same stamps were used for centuries and sometimes more than one foundry used the same stamp simultaneously.

Important bells may be listed for preservation by the diocese and their detailed history is often included in descriptive leaflets of the church.

Principal English Bellfoundries
1424-1513   Brasyers of Norwich, Norfolk
1506-1616   Newcombes of Leicester
1518-1709   Knights of Reading
1539-1741   Oldfields of Nottingham
1570-today   The Whitechapel Bell Foundry Ltd, London (incorporating Mot; Bartlet; Phelps; Lester; Pack; Mears; Mears & Stainbank)
1584-1697   Purdues of Somerset
1590-1682   Cliburys of Wellington, Shropshire
1610-1823   Penningtons of Devon and Cornwall
1631-1782   Bagleys of Chacombe, Northamptonshire
1635-1726   Chandlers of Drayton Parslow, Buckinghamshire
1652-1731   Smiths of York
1684-1830   Rudhalls of Gloucester
1698-1814   Bilbies of Chewstoke, Somerset
1788-1809/1853-1918   John Warner & Sons, London
1800-today   John Taylor & Co (Bellfounders) Ltd, Loughborough, Leicestershire
Always ask a trained ringer to lower the bell for examination and do not touch a bell set upside down or pull a rope attached to one.
For each bell take note of the name or number;
the note;
the weight;
the inscription;
the likely date;
the bellfounder;
the diameter of the mouth;
the presence of cannons and argent;
the condition
(cracked or sound);
and if rehung and by whom.

Argent — Head
Canons — Crown
Shoulder
Inscription band
Moulding
Wires
Waist
Soundbow
Lip

COMMUNION OR EUCHARIST: Cups

The Communion Wine
Before the Reformation, the cup at the centre of the Eucharist was known as a **chalice**; after about 1525 it was known as a **communion cup**, but the term chalice came back into common usage towards the end of the 18th century and for 19th and 20th century cups influenced by pre-Reformation designs.

The most ornate medieval chalices are about 17 cm high and set with **cabuchons**, whereas similar 19th century examples are larger and mounted with faceted jewels.

12th and 13th century Norman style chalice
Wide shallow bowl with moulded rim, sometimes shallower than illustrated and with everted rim.
Cylindrical stem, often quite plain.
Spherical knot, either lobed, wrythen, plain or pierced.
Circular foot with engraved or raised ornament *(other examples often have stamped beading on the edge).*

Font cup c. 1510
Font-shaped bowl on sturdy trumpet stem with narrow cabled collet at junction of bowl and stem. Bowl annulated by a band with raised inscription in plain roman capitals, *COMMUNION CUP*, the words separated by tied scrolls on a pounced ground, probably added in the 17th century.

Early 16th century pre-Reformation Tudor chalice
Deep bowl with everted rim, set in star-shaped calyx *(cup-like cavity)*
Hexagonal stem with vertical bands of rope moulding at each angle.
Gothic knot with six lozenge bosses, each with a tracery motif on red or green enamel on the facets, amidst intervening lobes.
Hexagonal lobed foot with saints in cusped niches engraved on the panels, one panel bearing an engraved crucifix.

METAL
Religious Objects

Tudor communion cup c. 1574
Deep bucket-shaped bowl, annulated with band of strapwork and moresques, resting on a compressed hemispherical knot above a wide flange.
Foot and base trumpet shaped, with stamped egg and dart moulding on edge.

Tudor communion cup c. 1576
Deep beaker-shaped bowl with everted rim decorated with strapwork arabesque.
Lozenge decorated collet joins bowl and spool stem with lozenge ornament at lower edge.
Central compressed knot.
Domed and stepped circular foot, the lower edge ornamented as on stem, the base encircled with gadrooning.

Communion cup c. 1600
Deep conical bowl engraved with IHS across the stem of a cross, within a sunburst.
Baluster stem.
High circular foot stepped at base with ring moulding.

Communion cup c. 1686
Deep beaker-shaped bowl with everted rim engraved with armorials on a lozenge, contained within foliate ornament of two crossed branches of laurel tied below with a ribbon.
Trumpet-shaped stem with narrow central flange
Shallow stepped and domed circular foot.
Inscriptions at this period usually in English in lettering similar to that used on contemporary monuments

Mid-18th century communion cup

Goblet-shaped bowl annulated with applied moulding above which is an engraved IHS within a sunburst and below inverted rays.

Trumpet-shaped stem with compressed moulded knot two-thirds of the way up and engraved putti at base. Domed and stepped foot with rayed decoration.

Late 18th century communion cup

Ogee-shaped bowl encircled near top with raised foliate ornament and festoons of flowers and foliage.
Fluted calyx reaching halfway up the bowl.
Baluster stem with spiral gadrooning.
Foliated collet joining the stem to the high domed fluted foot on a spreading base which is encircled with raised acanthus leaves.

Mid-19th century chalice

Hemispherical bowl annulated with lines of niello enclosing an inscription in 19th century lombardic lettering.
Small cast and applied calyx of fleurs-de-lys
Cylindrical stem with stepped mouldings and vertical wires and pellets on a niello ground.
Gadroons and foliated mouldings decorate the knot.
Filigree scrolls on the collet.
Conical foot divided into six panels by rope mouldings each containing an applied roundel with representations of the Evangelists, Agnus Dei and a Greek cross.
Stepped circular edge.

19th century chalice inspired by Norman style

Plain conical bowl set in an arcaded calyx, with filigree decorated architrave and spandrels, the pillars set with cabuchons.
Cylindrical stem annulated with mouldings above and below the angular knot which is decorated with filigree scrolling and 8 stone bosses.
High circular flaring foot with an inverted filigree arcade, as in the calyx, stepped and moulded edge to base, with a band of filigree ornament.

METAL
Religious Objects

20th century chalice
Double cone or egg-timer shape, the bowl shallower than the base.
Lower third of bowl and whole stem base decorated with hammered abstract geometrical designs.

Chalice
showing an amalgamation of decorative details from two silver gilt chalices of 1525 and 1527

Hemispherical bowl annulated with a band inscribed in gothic lettering on a hatched ground *CALICEM • SALUTARI • ACCIPIUM ET • NOMEN • INVOCABI* (sic).
Hexagonal collet of stepped moulding below the bowl and above the knot.
Hexagonal stem, rising from a balustrade with pinnacles at the angles, displaying panels of pierced quatrefoil tracery within cabling, interrupted by a large lobed Gothic knot with six projecting lozenge bosses embellished with raised human masks on the facets.
The panels of the high hexagonal foot are decorated in two stages, the upper with feathering, the lower with plain lettering on a hatched ground (indecipherable).
One bell-shaped panel, protruding from the others, is engraved with a crucifix, the rim of the bell curving onto the bottom step of a circular stepped flange.
Wavy-edged hexagonal stepped base with stamped vertical billet decoration on the riser.

THE SACRAMENT

Ciborium   covered receptacle for storing the consecrated Hosts, distinguishable from cup or chalice, when found without the cover, by rim or ledge (bezel) on which the cover rests.

Monstrance   decorative container for Sacrament to be displayed to worshippers.

Paten   plate on which the Sacrament is served during Eucharist.

Pyx   box for carrying the Sacrament to the sick

Salver   plate, larger than paten, for serving Sacrament during Eucharist

Tabernacle   decorative container for the ciborium or wafer box (see p. 11)

Tazza   wine cup with shallow circular bowl mounted on foot, often confused with patens or salvers.

Wafer box   box for storing the wafers

Ciborium
Baluster finial supporting a Patonce cross set with a white sapphire.

Slightly domed and stepped cover, *(which should be hallmarked)*

Shaped hemispherical bowl with everted rim.

Hexagonal collet at junction of bowl and hexagonal stem.
Stepped collet above and below a Wrythen pierced Gothic knot bearing six lozenge bosses with raised foliate ornament set with sapphire centres.

Stepped collet at junction of stem and hexagonal incurving foot.
Edge engraved with band of reeding
Six pierced trefoil toes

METAL
Religious Objects

THE SACRAMENT: Patens

Normally a simple flat decorated plate, the paten can have a foot and stem (**standing patens**) and certain 17th century covered patens are furnished with spool feet and covers and resemble ciboria. The covers of such standing patens are often an inverted copy of the base, known as **paten lids**, and were used in the 16th century to double as covers for the communion cup. The base of a paten is often decorated with a button bearing the Sacred Monogram or the name of the church in a roundel.

Paten 12th to 14th century

Circular with double depression.

Band contained within the moulded rim circumscribed in plain lombardic uncials on a hatched ground + *CALICEM SALUTARIS ACCIPIAM ET NOMINE DOMINE INVOCABO,* a cross at the beginning and lozenge devices between each word. Domed centre engraved with Head of Christ set in roundel within an engraved sunburst on a matted ground, all within an embossed sexfoil with spandrels engraved with small sun motifs. On the reverse, Sacred Monogram in Latin form.

Standing paten c.1576

Bezel to fit communion cup.

Spool foot, with button on base. Button engraved horizontally with date in arabic numerals. Reeded outer edge, similar to top.

Spool finial, outside annulated with a band of strapwork and moresques. Inside of paten lid undecorated with single depression and single reeded border to narrow rim, with protruding bezel.

Monstrance

Silver, parcel-gilt and set with carbuncles in the form of a shrine. Glazed crested roundel in the centre front, edged with rope moulding and fleurs-de-lys tracery, to contain the Sacrament. The roundel is supported on a stepped silver plinth with gilt moulding, engraved dog-tooth patterning and set with 5 carbuncles. On each side, a buttress decorated with tracery and geometric patterns, pinnacled and crocketed, with niches containing 2 gilt figures of angels holding crowns. Above the roundel, a gabled silver roof, with dormers, engraved with a sexfoil foliated device, set with carbuncles and with gilt cresting. A floriated gilt cross with central carbuncle at apex of roof.

Shrine rests on hexagonal stem decorated with engraved dog-tooth and other ornament, branching at top into scrolls and crockets and edged horizontally with brattishing. Compressed spherical knot with embossed lobes and 6 bosses, each framed in swirling crockets and set with a carbuncle. Gilt collet at junction of stem and foot. Hexfoil foot, parcel-gilt, decorated with foliate ornament on matted ground, with carbuncles set in each foil; the base with gilt mouldings and engraved decoration.

118

 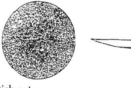

Salver c. 1693 used as a paten
Narrow rim with triple reeded border
Single depression with shallow straight-sided bouge.
Slight moulded collet at junction of top and high flaring foot which is edged with ovolo decoration and stands on a narrow flanged base.
Incised armorials in centre of well.
Marks are: London assay 1693; maker's mark PM within quatrefoil.
All marks are in the well except that of the lion passant which is on the underside of the flange. Underneath the salver is incised 1713.
Patens and salvers are often confused with tazzas which are deeper bodied wine cups.

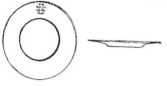

Plate paten
Broad rimmed plate with engraved patée cross on rim
Inscription engraved in roman capitals on back of rim

Dish paten
Saucer dish with shallow foot-rim
Hammered decoration covering inside

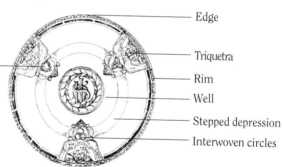

- Edge
- Triquetra
- Rim
- Well
- Stepped depression
- Interwoven circles

Circle within triangle

Alms dish
(usually large plate of base metal over 30cm diameter)
Circular silver alms dish with enamelled decoration (40.5 cm diameter), with moulded patterned edge to panelled rim.
3 medallions rise from bosses in stepped depression of the dish, containing embossed representations of The Holy Trinity (triquetra; circle within triangle; interwoven circles) framed by enamelled wing forms arching back to and framing silver reliefs of sailing ships on rim.
In the centre the Sacred Monogram IHS in plain roman capitals in a blue enamelled roundel within pink and white coiled rope pattern.

METAL
Religious Objects

Pyx
(vessel used to carry the Sacrament to the sick, usually a box smaller than a wafer box but found in many forms).

Wafer box
with lift out grid

Altar tabernacle in 3 stages
Crocketed pinnacle terminating in a foliated finial.

Open (to contain monstrance) with buttresses supporting hexagonal canopy, pinnacled and gabled.

Square base, each side with crocketed gable; door at front, decorated with raised cross set with crystals.
At the intersection Agnus Dei on an enamelled roundel.

Hanging tabernacle
with veil

CROSSES

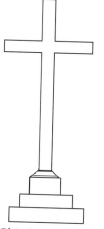

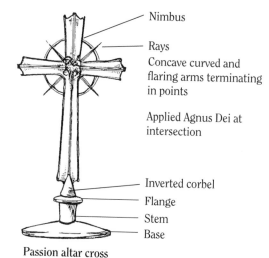

Nimbus

Rays

Concave curved and flaring arms terminating in points

Applied Agnus Dei at intersection

Inverted corbel

Flange

Stem

Base

Plain 3-stepped Latin Calvary altar cross

Passion altar cross

Processional cross Celtic-style
Handwrought brass wheel cross with repoussé Celtic ornament on the splayed limbs and wheel or nimbus.

Central concave sided lozenge medallion displaying Sacred Monogram IHS in plain roman letters on a chased ground. Spandrels of the nimbus similarly chased.

Compressed and annulated brass knot and cylindrical stem joins the cross to the screw-jointed oak stem with brass ferrule at base.

Screw joint

Pectoral cross
incorporating rose and heart emblems in gold and enamel

Brass ferrule

METAL
Religious Objects

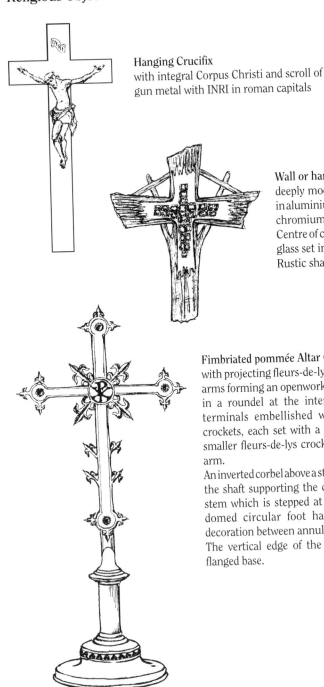

Hanging Crucifix
with integral Corpus Christi and scroll of
gun metal with INRI in roman capitals

Wall or hanging cross
deeply modelled and textured
in aluminium alloy with bright
chromium plated finish.
Centre of coloured faceted slab
glass set in epoxy resin.
Rustic shape with silhouette.

Fimbriated pommée Altar Cross
with projecting fleurs-de-lys at the angels of the
arms forming an openwork nimbus. A Chi Rho
in a roundel at the intersection. The four
terminals embellished with 3 fleurs-de-lys
crockets, each set with a jewel. Two pairs of
smaller fleurs-de-lys crockets adorn the lower
arm.
An inverted corbel above a stepped flange attaches
the shaft supporting the cross to a cylindrical
stem which is stepped at the base. The high
domed circular foot has a band of trefoil
decoration between annulations on the dome.
The vertical edge of the foot has a moulded
flanged base.

Mid-19th century Crucifix

The arms are engraved with fleurs-de-lys in diaper pattern. To each arm is attached a quatrefoil edged with roll moulding, engraved with foliage on a matted ground, set with a single amethyst. The 3 upper arms terminate in fleurs-de-lys with roll mouldings and engraved foliage centres. The intersection of the arms, outlined with gables of roll moulding but otherwise left plain as a background to the head and arms of Christ, is surrounded by an octagon, cusped on its inner side, concave on its outer and crested on the 4 exposed angles with fleurs-de-lys, the width filled with a band of dog-tooth ornament between roll mouldings on a hatched ground *(for figure see page 53)*.

An inverted corbel is placed at the junction of the cross and the knot of the annulated cylindrical stem. The compressed annulated spherical knot has 4 bosses bearing applied roundels of fleurs- de-lys on blue enamel.

The high tapering foot is engraved with the Sacred Monogram IHS, on a hatched ground within a roundel, a cursive band of engraved trefoils follows the wavy four-lobed edge.

An engraved band of hatching occupies the space between the edge of the foot and the base. The frame of the cross is of wood cased on the front in plates of base metal, the base is of electroplated base metal and the figure of Christ is electrogilt.

METAL
Religious Objects

LECTERNS
Lecterns became a feature of post-Reformation churches, usually very austere and made up of an amalgamation of different decorative parts. From the beginning of the 19th century lecterns became more simple. **Book stands** are particularly used to support the priest's **missal** during services.

Brass lectern c. 1683
Book desk in form of an eagle with outstretched wings flanked by single bracket candle holders with glass tulip-shaped shades, standing on a sphere which is supported on a flaring concave section above various bands of moulding including some raised leaf work.
Baluster stem with a stepped circular base.
Cylindrical section springing from stepped moulding above the high-domed lectern base resting of four lion séjant feet.

Late 19th century brass lectern
Double desk with gable ends pierced with cusped circular openings and band of cresting across top.
Cylindrical stem decorated with rings of red and blue inlaid mastic with formalised leaf forms supporting the desk.
Central compressed spherical knot with attached band with knobbed decoration, scalloped edges and trefoil collets above and below.
Trefoil collet at junction of stem and base
Conical base which is decorated with pierced sexfoils and rings of red and blue inlaid mastic.
Stands on 4 red painted paw feet (which have been restored) protruding from the cusped edge.

Pedestal type missal or book stand
in highly polished brass with
revolving bookplate embellished with
pierced quatrefoils within roundels
in the corners, and a central roundel
with Sacred Monogram IHS in Latin
form on punched ground.
Rope moulded edge to bookplate,
screwjoint and trumpet base.

Ledger type missal or book stand
with cast scrolled and foliated end
panels and scalloped edge to
bookplate ledge.

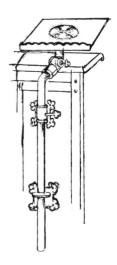

Pulpit desk
with quatrefoil decoration in centre
and a scalloped ledge.
Adjustable stem (by use of key)
attached to inside of pulpit drum by
clips to square bracket plates with
trefoil corners.

METAL

METAL
Religious Objects

PROCESSIONAL

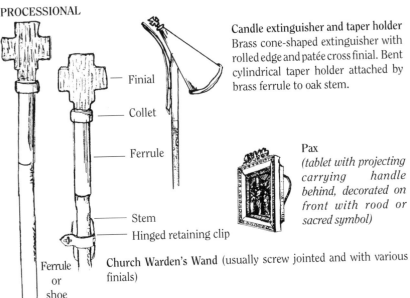

— Finial

— Collet

— Ferrule

— Stem

— Hinged retaining clip

Ferrule
or
shoe

Church Warden's Wand (usually screw jointed and with various finials)

Candle extinguisher and taper holder
Brass cone-shaped extinguisher with rolled edge and patée cross finial. Bent cylindrical taper holder attached by brass ferrule to oak stem.

Pax
(tablet with projecting carrying handle behind, decorated on front with rood or sacred symbol)

Verger's wand *(similar to Church Warden's but shorter)*

Morse
(badge sewn or pinned to band joining sides of cope, sometimes embroidered but usually metal)
Holy Trinity in basse-taille enamel (see p. 101) on silver with pierced gold outer rim.

Pastoral staff or crozier
Silver gilt, decorated with enamels and semi-precious stones.
Hexagonal crook, imbricated and set with stones, terminating in serpent's head with forked tongue. The curve is connected to the stem by a foliated ornament.
Central figures of Christ (standing) charging St Peter (seated) on an enamelled ground.
4 marks above niches, maker's mark, sterling standard, Assay Office and date.
Flanking the stem are 2 tiers of niches, separated by pinnacled buttresses, occupied by figures of saints and bishops under foliated canopies; upper tier is surmounted by 3 more figures standing against alternate facets of the hexagonal stem.
Plinth of the lower tier of niches is set on a foliated boss rising, by a concave stem, from a knot decorated with swirling gadroons.
A shield, bearing the arms of the See, is set on the ferrule of the oak staff.

GATES AND RAILINGS

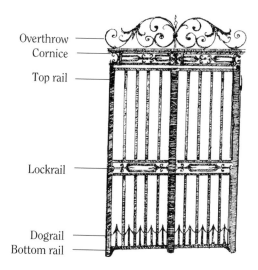

Overthrow
Cornice
Top rail

Lockrail

Dograil
Bottom rail

17th century wrought iron gates (pair)
Overthrow of 2 large bifurcated S scrolls, passing
through central collar and decorated with small scrolls
including fiddle head, flat penny nibs and pair of well
placed waterleaves.
Frieze of strapwork between 2 square section rails
below cornice.
Plain square section top rail
Double lockrail with strapwork frieze
Plain square section bottom rail with dograil of
arrowheads.
In each gate there are 4 square section verticals,
between unadorned stiles, the verticals being mortised,
tenoned and welded through the horizontals.

16th century wrought iron tomb railing
Fleur-de-lys alternating with spiked finials to the
uprights which change to flat section above the
toprail.
Main verticals with ball and steeple finials,
ornamented with double bar twist below the toprail.

METAL
Practical Objects

LIGHTING

Candlesticks

17th century pewter candlestick
Bell-shaped

17th century brass candlestick
Vertical slot in cylindrical stem with protruding candle ejector.
Drip pan in centre of stem.
Wide spreading base.

Late 17th century silver or gilt Baroque style candlestick
Gadrooned drip pan and pricket.
Baluster stem shaped and ornamented.
Scrolled tripod base surmounted by putti.

Classical silver candlestick c.1675
Fluted and reeded column of Doric form with broad platform at base.
High waisted plinth.
Large square stepped foot.

Early 18th century silver or brass candlestick
Steel rod ejector in base.
Reel-shaped sconce on distinct neck.
Shouldered baluster stem with knots.
Moulded and depressed polygonal foot.

Neo-classical style silver or brass late 18th century candlestick
Tapering fluted stem.
High trumpet-shaped foot.
Bell shaped leaf - decorated sconce with separate nozzle.

Nozzle and drip pan scalloped, with deep indentations between each pair of scallops, annulated with two paris of incised rings.

Cylindrical stem with 3 knots, the upper one gem set and chased with zigzag ornament, the lower little more than a flange.

Stem between them annulated by double rows of incised rings enclosing a zigzag pattern.

Large compressed central knot, chased and decorated with bead mouldings and with stones as bosses.

Stem decorated as above, with rings and zigzag pattern.

Moulded collets
High conical foot
Panels formed of chased lines with stones set in high collets.

Pierced cusped openings alternating with pierced roundels.

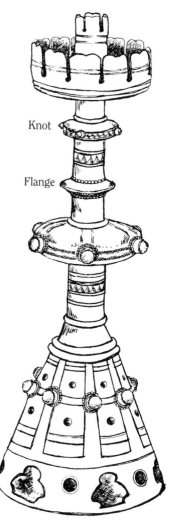

Knot

Flange

19th century altar copper gilt candlestick set with semi-precious stones

METAL

METAL
Practical Objects

Five-branch candelabrum

Brass flat-scrolled branches with ivy leaf repoussé ornament springing from top of cylindrical stem, holding shallow saucer-shaped grease-pans with scalloped cresting and annulated cylindrical nozzles. Central fifth socket at top of reeded rod with scrolling brackets.

Polychrome imbricated iron stem with brass terminal ferrule, passing through collar of base and joined, by a brass knot, at top to a brass cylindrical stem.

Wrought iron tripod base formed of broken scrolled legs with ribbon ends, united by wide incurving collar with bolt-end terminals.

Highly polished brass processional torch or bier light
(135 cm h. to pan)
Incurving 4 sided tapering drip pan with plain cylindrical socket. Cylindrical stem with 2 compressed and stepped knots
Removable 4 sided incurving and tapering base on 4 bun feet.

Flowerstand
(adapted from torchere)
Disc top with embattled gallery.
Twist stem joined by spindle collet to rectangular section supported by scrolled cruciform bracket feet united to stem by clip collars in 3 places.

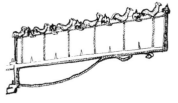

16th century wrought iron bracket of prickets, attached to wall and pivoted
2 horizontal bars, connected by spiral uprights, forming 5 open panels with spike at midpoint of base of each as support for candle which passes through ring in upper bar, crested with alternating fleurs-de-lys and cocks.

METAL

130

Branch candelabrum

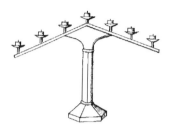

Pyramid style candelabrum
with hexagon base

Rushlight holder

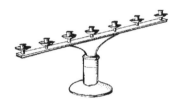

Strap sconce

Slant style candelabrum
with round base

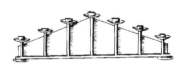

Seven branch jerusalem candlestick
or menorah

Delta branch candelabrum

14th century wrought iron herse *(top)*
erected around or over tombs for their
protection with fleur-de-lys decorated
candle prickets

METAL
Practical Objects

Votive stand
Stove-enamel finish, 33 lights, slide-out tray.

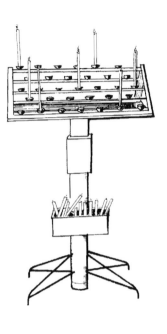

Votive stand
Wrought iron, 16 lights, aluminium drip pans with brass pickets.

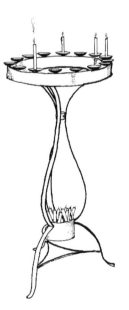

Either of these stands may be fitted with sanctum lights or glasses

Hanging lights

Lanterns and chandeliers in churches were used to supplement candlesticks from around 1600, first plain English chandeliers and later in the century, more ornate Dutch examples.

The commonest shape of 17th century chandelier has drooping branches hooked into rings in the balusters or into trays pierced with holes. The branches are mostly circular in section and of two opposed curves with moulding at the join, so that the inner end forms an open spiral and the outer end is everted. The finial at the top was often highly decorative and different provincial centres had their own characteristic finials.

During the 18th century, the arms became shorter, drooped less and were fitted to the circumference of a flatter central sphere. The branches themselves were more elaborate, often hexagonal or octagonal in section and covered with scrolling. The spaces between the branches and tiers were filled with ornament, usually gadrooning and the most popular finial was a flame. Dutch chandeliers in the 18th century had no finials or ornament and the branches were attached to hollow trays by tenons and pins, rather than hooks. Chandeliers made from 1600 to 1900 have solid arms where as 20th century chandeliers have hollow arms to take the electrical wiring.

Brass chandelier of mixed date

Top finial

London dove finial
(Bristol dove has closed wings and no feathers on body)

Shaft of ball and baluster turnings (hollow and held together by an iron hanging rod)

Tiers of curving branches, usually 2 or 3

Pendant finial

Oil lamp

with clear glass chimney and opaque china hemispherical shade.
Brass body fitting into an annulated iron girdle to which are attached 3 wrought iron broken-scrolled brackets suspended from iron link chains.

METAL
Practical Objects

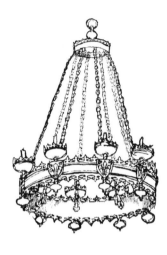

Wrought iron corona lucis

Hanging by chains from circlet crested with fleurs-de-lys.

Bowl drip pans under 8 candle sockets similarly ornamented and attached to outer side of coronet by twist stems with pendant turnip-shaped finials, the joins hidden by applied fleur-de-lys decorated shields, painted red and gold.

Rims of annulated coronet decorated with fleurs-de-lys.

Sanctuary lamp

Highly polished brass with cast and finely modelled Dolphin arms attached by their tails to a ball and baluster pendant finial of the drip-pan, by their snouts to the socket in which an eight day type ruby glass cylindrical funnel with everted lip rests, and by their dorsal fins to three chains hanging from a brass circlet surmounted with a ring similar to that at the base of the pendant finial.

Describe the shape and ornament of every part and the way the light is fitted together. For chandeliers, record the number of tiers, the number of branches in each tier and the finials.

Bracket Lights

Brass candle sconce
Cartouche-shaped sconce with repoussé decoration and central uninscribed cartouche, lower part reeded and fluted.
Simple knotted s-shaped arm of round section springing from a floriated boss at the base of the sconce, holding plain saucer-shaped drip pan with annulated cylindrical nozzle moulded at rim.

Brass candle bracket
Horizontal rod of square section interrupted by twists, emerging from fleurette on backplate, supported above and below by inward scrolling waterleaf brackets, terminating in trefoil.
Floral collar near terminal is threaded with stem of urn- shaped socket.

19th century wrought iron hexagonal porch lantern
Baluster finial with attached ring
Double domed cover with ogee ribs and scrolled-over lower edge, pierced panels with whorls (lower dome) and lozenges (upper dome).
Band with rectangular piercing between domes.
Tapering glazed panels with iron traceried glazing bars in heads fixed to scrolled-over crested upper rail with band of pierced arcading between scroll and scrolled-over lower edge of cover.
Pendant finial of scrolled brackets radiating from centre to plain moulded outside edges of bottom rail of glazed panels.

METAL

Brass bracket gasolier
Band of floral engraving on the globe which sits in a trefoil crested socket with acorn pendant finial.
Waterleaf decorated scrolled arm with cast brass fleurette inner terminal to the scroll-end near wall plate.
Scroll end linked to waterleaf stem.

Sanctuary bracket lamp
Bright polished chromium plate with glass funnel nestling in calyx above disc set on flaring reeded stem sitting in a collar at the end of a shaped triangular wall bracket.

Processional torch
Chromium plated brass torch on teak stem with clear glass cylindrical funnel. A handle-grip of textured brass to prevent it slipping through collar of wall mounted bracket.

TANKARDS, FLAGONS AND JUGS

Beaker   shaped, lipped vessel without a handle or a stem
Cup   term applied to any form of drinking vessel in old documents
Flagon   large vessel from which other vessels are filled
Mug   cylindrical drinking vessel without lid
Tankard   drinking vessel with handle and hinged lid

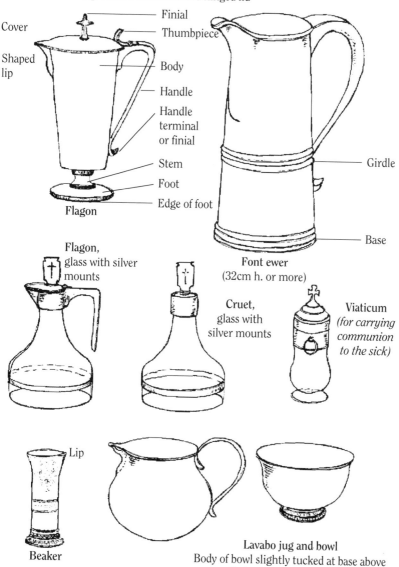

Cover
Finial
Thumbpiece
Shaped lip
Body
Handle
Handle terminal or finial
Stem
Foot
Edge of foot
Flagon

Girdle
Base

Font ewer
(32cm h. or more)

Flagon, glass with silver mounts

Cruet, glass with silver mounts

Viaticum (for carrying communion to the sick)

Lip
Beaker

Lavabo jug and bowl
Body of bowl slightly tucked at base above applied spreading gadrooned foot

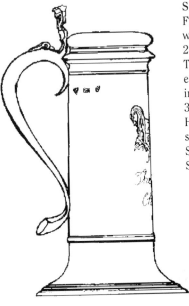

Silver flagon c. 1630
Flat cap lid with moulded thumbpiece pierced with heart motif.
2 marks only (assay and date) inside lid.
Tall cylindrical body with boldly cast lip, engraved on front with armorials and inscription in contemporary script.
3 marks by handle (sterling, assay and date)
Hollow scroll handle of tapering form with simple shield-shaped finial.
Spreading skirt foot with moulded band above.
Stepped and moulded edge to base.

James I pewter flagon, c. 1610
with knopped lid; ridged, erect thumbpiece. Plain strap handle. Slightly tapering body with moulded foot. The bottom of the drum of the flagon is curved and does not touch the surface on which the flagon stands, the moulded foot performing that function. *(In a few cases a flat base has been fixed across the bottom of the foot).*

Spire pewter flagon, c. 1720-1800
Knopped and domed cover
Tapering body
Curved solid thumbpiece
S-shaped handle
Domed foot
Double fillet just above base

METAL

Britannia metal (pewter) flagon c. 1790-1900
Domed lid
Palmate thumbpiece
Scroll handle
Large spout
Slightly tapering drum
Several fillets near gently curving flange foot

19th century flagon with pear-shaped ruby glass body and electrogilt mounts
High domed mount attached to hinged cover (with trefoil thumbpiece) decorated with row of tracery edged with rope moulding and cresting of trefoils surrounding wire-work nest supporting Pelican in her Piety. Plain lip, triangular in section projecting from band of engraved vine ornament. Scroll handle with mouchette tracery in roundel and bifurcated terminal.

Upper mount annulated with roll moulding and pendant cut-card fleurs-de-lys below frieze of quatrefoil tracery surmounted by inscription CHRIST SO LOVED US in plain roman capitals enclosed by roll mouldings on hatched ground.

Engraved metal roundel edged with cut-card trefoils enclosing the Sacred Monogram IHS on front of pear-shaped ruby glass body between mounts which encase upper and lower parts. Lower mount annulated with roll moulding surmounted by cut-card fleurs-de-lys.

High quatrefoil foot with moulded edge engraved with crosses within roundels hatched as for inscription.

Hourglass stands

17th century
swordrest

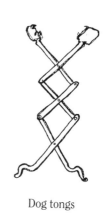

Dog tongs

METAL

COINS AND MEDALS
Both the side with the monarch's head (obverse) and the decorative side (reverse) are of interest and can be recorded with a rubbing.

JEWELLERY
Jewels set in 19th and 20th century church plate are likely to be facetted whereas earlier gems are usually cabuchon.

Cabuchon	stone of rounded natural form, polished but not cut
Cameo	two layers of glass, the top layer cut in relief to reveal the underlayer
Carbuncle	bright red stone
Facet	one side of cut gem
Filigree	gold or silver wire or pellets applied to gold or silver base in ornamental patterns
Girandole	openwork clasp of alternating ribbon and bow design set with stones
Intaglio	gem with incised design

PAPER
Prints and Paintings

A miscellany of objects in churches may be made of paper or have paper as their chief material. In addition, certain framed objects dealt with under WOOD, for example, **The Roll of Honour**, may in fact appear on paper. **Paintings** are dealt with here though their chief material is most often canvas not paper.

FRAMED OBJECTS

All kinds of framed paper objects will be found in churches, invariably hung on the wall. The most interesting features of all framed objects will be the name of the artist, the date of the work, its subject matter and, in the case of maps and architectural drawings, its scale.

Architectural drawings	give vital clues to changes in the church's development; interesting to compare with appearance today.
Drawings & watercolours	often of religious scenes, of the church, or local landscape.
Certificates	usually framed
List of Vicars	often framed manuscript, or painted on wood or stone
Painting	most likely to be copy of religious work, sometimes well known, in ornate frame which may be interesting, if old.
Photographs	the date, the sitter and the photographer may be interesting.
Prints	impression in ink on paper, usually framed but may be unframed. Often engravings of contemporary works of art, giving the artist's name alongside the engraver's.
Roll of Honour	list of members of parish who fought in World War I 1914-18 and World War II 1939-45, usually framed and glazed and may be illuminated with regimental badges.
Stamps	often found amongst faculties and correspondence, most interesting when on envelopes with indication of date.
Vignette	small picture without defined borders

PRINTS

Technical terms used in the lettering are usually in Latin or French with abbreviations and contemporary spelling. There are three main recognisable types:

Intaglio	line, steel, stipple engraving; etching; dry point and aquatint
Relief or relievo	woodcuts or wood engravings
Lithographic	printing from stone; resembles drawing with very soft pencil
Laid down	anything pasted on paper
Original engraving	engraved by the artist
Proof	signed by the artist and the engraver
Proof before letters	unsigned, the name of the artist and engraver printed
Lettered proof	title of subject, name of artist, engraver and publisher printed

INSCRIPTIONS

comp.	composuit	designed by
del., fig., gez.	delineavit, figuravit, dessine, gezeichnet	drawn by
exc., imp.	excudit, impressit	printed by
fac., fec., inc.,	fecit, incidit, sculpsit, grave	printed by
inv.,	invenit	indicates original artist
pinx., ping.,	pinxit, peint	painted by

PAPER
Books and bookbinding

Most church documents are now deposited in the county record office, where enquirers can usually view them on request. A series of books, mostly in current use, will, however, be kept in the church, in the church chest, belfry or vestry, or possibly in the rectory.

BOOKS AND PUBLICATIONS FOUND IN CHURCHES

Faculty	authorisation from Diocesan Chancellor (or from 1993, Archdeacon) for alteration or addition to the church. It may give date and names of architect/designer, donor, and materials.
Library	many churches have a library of ecclesiastical works.
Minute Book	record of meetings of parochial church council (ecclesiastical) not to be confused with parish council (civil).
Missal	earlier name for service book used at Eucharist. If large, for use of priest at altar.
Register	record of baptisms, marriages, and burials, sometimes in the same volume.
Terrier	record of lands, goods and possessions of parish church.
Visitors' Book	record of visitors to the church from outside the parish.

Other books found are registers of services, gift books, war memorial books, village histories, bibles, prayer books and other service books; sheet music; descriptive leaflets; parish magazines.

TERMS

Association copy	book associated by ownership or annotation with the author, or with someone connected with the author.
Backbone	spine of book
Bands (raised)	ridges on spine caused by the sewing cords, or added (flat) in imitation for decoration.
Binding	covering of outside boards of book
Blind tooled	impressions stamped without gold infill
Boards	sides of bound or cased book
Bolts	folds which have to be cut before the pages can be read
Bookplate or ex libris	owner's identification label, usually pasted inside front cover; may be early, eg. heraldic, or designed by interesting artist.
Boss	knob of brass or other metal fastened on boards for protection of binding or for decoration.
Call-mark	see Shelf-mark
Cartouche	loosely applied to round, oval or decorated labels and bookplates
Case-bound	book cover made completely before being attached
Clasp	hinged catch for holding together the two covers of the book
Colophon	in early printed books, a statement of the printer's name, date and place of publication at the end of the book, later superseded by title page; it may include publisher's imprint or device.
Deckle	rough natural edge of hand-made paper.
Dedication copy	presented by author to person to whom the book is dedicated
Dentelle	border of lacy pattern on inner edge

Doublure	edge of binding turned in and visible, often decorated; can als mean lining of silk, etc, replacing endpapers
Dust cover or jacket	protective loose paper cover
Enclosures	any material not part of the book but inserted in it (eg. letters pictures, cuttings).
Endpapers	leaves of plain or ornamental paper added by binder, one hal of each (the paste-down) being attached to the inside of th cover, and the other (the flyleaf) loose.
Ex libris	see Bookplate
Fillet	tooled line on cover
Finishing	lettering and decoration
Fleuron	flower-shaped device stamped on bindings, often at corners
Flyleaf	see Endpapers
Fore-edge	edge opposite spine; fore-edge paintings show when the fore edge is spread out.
Format	statement indicative of shape, size and make-up of book, (eg octavo, folio etc).
Foxing	freckle-like brownish spots on paper caused by damp
French grooves	deep concave joints between spine and boards
Gauffering	gilt edges decorated with finishing tools
Guards	folded strips of paper sewn or pasted into the back durin rebinding.
Gutter	adjoining inside margins of page
Head and tail	top and bottom of spine
Headpiece	printed ornament or illustration at head of chapter or section see also Vignette
Headband	in early or fine binding: protective beading worked in sil thread at head and tail; in modern binding: pasted strip glue on for decoration.
Headcap	leather at top and tail of spine, drawn out to cover the headban
Hollow-backed	binding method in which spine is attached to a paper tube; se Tight backed
Horae or Book of Hours	manuscript or printed collection of the monastic day office and prayers for private use.
Inscribed	copy autographed by the author, usually at the request of th owner.
Label (skiver)	thin pieces of morocco (even on a calf book) with lettering From 1750 paper labels were applied to paper spines
Limited edition	usually individually numbered, often by hand
Manuscript	book or document written by hand
Marbling	process of colouring endpapers in variegated patterns based o patterns in marble.
Mint condition	as good as new
Octavo (8vo)	leaf of paper folded 3 times, ie. into 8, usually between 15 25cm high.
Panel	rectangle formed of single or multiple fillets, gilt or blind stamped on boards or between bands on spine.

Panel stamp	leather bindings decorated in blind with a large stamping tool.
Paperback	book without hard covers; cover may nowadays be synthetic material or glazed paper.
Perfect binding	(or **rubber-back** or **glue-back**) book made in **sections** but held together by adhesive.
Plate	illustration printed separately and sometimes on different paper from the text.
Presentation copy	spontaneous gift of the author, the value lying in the interest of the recipient or his connection with the author.
Provenance	pedigree of book's previous ownership
Quarto (4to)	leaf of paper folded twice, ie. into 4, usually 25 & 40cm high.
Recto	right hand page
Repairs	books may be re-backed, re-joined, re-margined, re-set.
Rotulus	book in roll form
Roll-stamp	cylindrical tool cut in relief to repeat its designs in rotation.
Rubric	instruction or heading introducing sections of text; (originally a capital letter distinguished by red ink).
Sections	folded sheets of paper, usually of 4 or 8 leaves or multiples thereof, from which the book is made up.
Semis	repeating pattern made with small tools (**seme**)
Shelf-mark	group of numbers or letters indicating place on library shelf; may provide clue to original owner.
Signature	letter or numeral at foot of page to indicate sequence of sheets; see also **Section**
Stamped	impressed with gold or left blind
Tailpiece	printed ornament or illustration at end of chapter or book, see **Vignette**
Tight-backed or fast-backed:	binding method in which spine is attached directly to the back of the sections; see **Hollow-backed**
Title page	page at beginning giving particulars of title, authorship, date, publisher, place, etc.
Tooling	decoration of cover by hand tools
Uncut	edges left uncut by rebinding (not to be confused with bolts).
Verso	left hand page
Vignette	illustration without a border, often used as head-or tail piece.
Watermark	mark in paper visible when held to light and helpful in dating printing.

PAPER

PAPER
Books and bookbinding

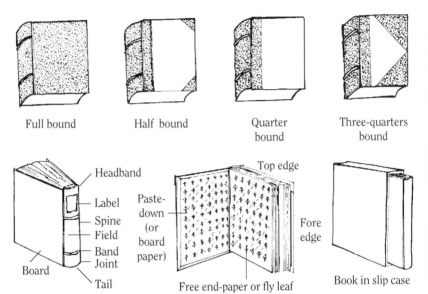

Full bound   Half bound   Quarter bound   Three-quarters bound

Headband, Label, Spine, Field, Band, Joint, Board, Tail

Paste-down (or board paper)

Top edge, Fore edge

Free end-paper or fly leaf

Book in slip case

BINDINGS

Armorial	stamped with a coat of arms, possibly added at a later date. Royal arms do not necessarily denote royal ownership, even if the book is dedicated to a royal personage.
Calf	smooth, without grain, can be variously treated and coloured.
Etruscan	classical decoration of urn, stylized palm leaves, or key decoration.
Fanfare style:	
Forel binding	parchment dressed to look like vellum
Irish	paper lozenge label in centre of board
Mosaic	polychrome decoration of binding by use of paint, onlays or inlays.
Parchment	usually sheep or goat, prepared for writing or painting
Publishers cloth	apart from paperback, the usual style of commercial binding, introduced in 1823.
Rococo	c-shaped curves and shell decoration popular in the late 1770's and 1780's.
Russia leather	rich, smooth cowhide, scented, often decorated with blind lozenge pattern.
Scots binding	wheel pattern
Signed binding	binder's or designer's name or initials forming part of design.
Sombre binding	black leather, tooled in blind, popular 1675-1725
Spanish calf	bold dashes of red and green acid on calf binding
Tree calf	calf binding with sides stained to resemble trees or foliage
Vellum	very fine parchment or calf
Yapp binding	limp leather with overlapping edges (from 19th century bookseller's name).

PAPER

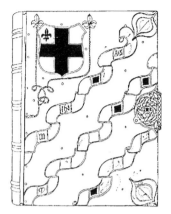

Red leather binding with silver panels on both covers

Upper cover:	3 bands of spiralling ribbon decoration with moulded edges and set with enamels bearing Sacred Monograms on copper (all much worn), descending diagonally from R to L.
	On top L corner, an enamelled shield with coat of arms (Arg. a cross Gu. in dexter chief a fleur-de-lys Az.) surrounded by rope moulding with fleur-de-lys finials flanking the shield at the top.
	Raised lobed bosses at top and bottom R corners.
Lower cover:	8 inset enamels on copper
	In top R corner an enamelled swan with motto below, surrounded by rope moulding.
	Raised lobed bosses at top and bottom L corners
	Brass clasp with roundel of mouchette tracery on upper cover.

BIBLES:

Every church will have at least one copy of the Bible, it is most likely to be one of the following:

Great Bible:	1539 - 1541, 7 editions, re-printing ceased 1569
Cranmer's Bible	1540, long preface by Archbishop Cranmer
Breeches Bible	1560, roman type, see Genesis, chap III, v.7
Authorised Version	1611
Revised Version	1881, 1884, 1895 (parts)
Two Version edition	1900

Essential information is author, title, place of publication (if other than London) publisher and date. Note the illustrator, format, page height, binding, inscriptions and other marks if the volume is of special interest.

Format: (for book) *A N AUTHOR, Title of book, Publisher, Town, Date* (for article in journal) *A N AUTHOR, 'Title of article', 'Title of journal' vol. xxx, 1976, pp. 36-41* (for information taken from a church leaflet) *name and location of church, nth edition, 1977.*

STONE
Terms

Churches were often the earliest stone buildings in the community. The majority are still stone built, although other materials, such as brick, flint or concrete, have been used for churches where they are common as a local building material or where fashion demands. Decorative features found in stone will be similar in other building materials.

Ornamental stonework is often an important aspect of the decoration of a church, so that, although much of the appropriate terminology is strictly architectural *(see ARCHITECTURE)*, identification should be easier by reference to stone features in this chapter. Certain features, including **pulpits, feretories and screens**, are more likely to be wooden than stone in Britain and are therefore treated in the chapter on *WOOD*.

Aumbry	cupboard, usually for the Reserved Sacrament, in north wall of chancel (see p. 11)
Chamfer	the narrow surface formed when an angle is cut away obliquely. It may be moulded, concave *(hollow)*, sunk or stopped.
Credence	table or shelf near the altar, usually on the south side.
Easter sepulchre	canopied recess in north chancel wall, similar to a tomb chest, used to contain the Sacrament or effigy of Christ between Good Friday and Easter Morning. Occasionally of wood.
Mensa	stone altar-top incised with five consecration crosses.
Pillar piscina	piscina on pillar, freestanding or against wall.
Piscina	basin with drain, used for washing sacred vessels, set into wall, sill or floor south of an altar.
Sedilia (s. sedile)	seats for clergy, generally on south side of chancel.
Squint	aperture pierced through wall to allow view of altar.
Stoup	receptacle for holding holy water often in the form of a deeply dished stone set in a niche or on a pillar near a doorway.

Stone brackets
for statues or statuettes

Pillar piscina

Corbel

Credence shelf

Mensa

Cresset stone
(Stone with cup-like hollows filled with oil and floating wicks to give light for those performing night duties in church) (rare today)

Piscina

Squint

Aumbry

Bread oven

**14th century
Easter sepulchre**
Canopied recess of 3 bays with crocketed, pinnacled and cusped ogee arches, above a shelf, resembling a tomb chest with 4 panels of similar blind arched decoration. Adjacent on the west side is a floor level tomb recess of similar date and style.

**14th century
Sedilia in range with Piscina**
Cusped cinquefoiled ogee heads with crockets and finials.
Detached cylindrical shafts, with moulded capitals and bases, separating 3 stepped seats and piscina.

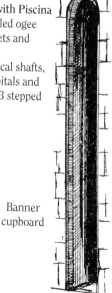

Banner cupboard

13th century sedilia

Statue niche (empty)

STONE
Fonts

Saxon drum or tub font
with lead-lined bowl decorated with crudely carved Latin crosses within arcading.
Two bands of cable moulding above the stepped base.

Norman pedestal font
with square bowl, in form of capital with roundels containing carved patterns alternating with large heads at corners. Short octagonal stem springing from drum pedestal on octagonal plinth.
Remains of iron staple on rim for locking flat cover.

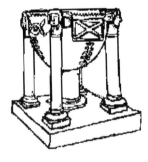

Norman table font
with cup bowl, elaborately carved with chevron design around rim and with geometric motifs and stiff-leaf on body, supported on massive central cylindrical stem.
4 angle shafts, rising from square plinth, outside the bowl, support projecting mask capitals against the sides of top of the bowl.

Early English font
Lead-lined hemispherical bowl, annulated with a band of continuous tendrils of foliage, carved in high relief, placed just below the rim. Plain cylindrical stem descends to a spreading foot, embellished with stylized acanthus leaves in high relief. Mounted on a millstone plinth.

18th century font

Lead-lined bowl with a band of carved decoration around the rim; made up of four cherubs' heads with swags of drapery between. Below the rim the bowl tapers in a concave curve to a gadrooned calyx in high relief.

Octagonal baluster stem with a band of carved anthemion leaves around the base. Stepped and moulded octagonal pedestal set on a shallow plinth.

Late 19th century font (1873),

copied from 15th century font
Octagonal bowl with carved representations of the 4 Evangelists and their attributes, alternating with kneeling angels, each under a crocketed ogee canopy in the panels.

Bosses of demi-angels at points of intersection beneath pinnacled buttresses which separate the panels.

Octagonal stem ornamented with shields bearing symbols of the Passion on panels between engaged shafts.

Oakleaf motifs in covered section beneath bowl.

The moulded bases of the shafts stand on a stepped octagonal plinth standing on large stepped and moulded cruciform plinth of Mansfield stone.

STONE

TEXTILES
Terms

All sorts of textiles are encountered in churches, some connected with church ritual, others with decoration or even the comfort of the congregation. Vestments are dealt with under *COSTUME* but all other ecclesiastical textiles, including cloths, veils and kneelers are considered here.

Since textiles in churches often involve work of devotion, specialist techniques, particularly embroidery and tapestry, are common on small scale objects like kneelers and on large scale objects like wall hangings, popular in modern churches. Fine quality materials were used for textiles in churches from the earliest times.

FABRICS

Brocade	generally silk, but may be gold, cotton or synthetic. Woven with a raised pattern of coloured threads. Used for vestments, frontals and curtains.
Cloth of gold	fabric with gold thread woven into the cloth.
Cloth of silver	fabric with silver thread woven into the cloth.
Cotton	any fabric from fine muslin to heavy canvas woven from the fibres of the cotton plant. Today generally used for altar linen and surplices.
Damask	reversible, usually monochrome, with a self-pattern either abstract or of monograms, dates, arms etc. Linen damask used for towels; cotton and wool for curtains, pew seats etc.; silk for vestments and frontals.
Garniture	fringes, tassels, knots, cords, etc.
Lace	fine open fabric made by hand or machine
Linen	woven from the fibres of flax. Cool to touch and slightly shiny. Originally always used for altar linen.
Lurex	a metal-coloured thread/fabric much used today instead of genuine gold thread in church embroidery.
Silk	woven from the thread produced by the larvae of the bombycine moth. Woven into many rich fabrics used for vestments, frontals etc.
Synthetics	man made fabrics, woven from thread produced in a laboratory. Will not crease, so the thread often added to natural fibres as well as used on its own.
Suede	pigskin, common in 20th century appliqué work.
Velvet	silk or cotton thread woven into a pile.

DECORATIVE TECHNIQUES

Applied work or appliqué the attaching of different fabrics, colours and shapes to a ground fabric.

Crewel work decorative embroidery with coloured wools on plain linen or twill ground.

Canvas work any type of stitch worked into holed canvas. This is **not** tapestry.

Crochet found in churches in the form of crochet lace, used as edging for communion cloths, super frontals and, sometimes, vestments.

Gold work the richest form of embroidery, using thread of fine gold paper wound round a core of silk. Other gold threads made from gold wire are:-

Purl	like a coiled spring
Bullion	large purl
Passing	fine gold wire
Pearl purl	tiny gold beads
Plate	flat strips
Spangles	thin pieces of shiny metal with a small hole for attachment.

Patchwork similar to inlaid but with symmetrical pieces.

Quilting two or more layers of material held together by stitched pattern, sometimes with cord inserted.

Tapestry fabric with a pictorial design, woven by a different technique from that of woven cloth. Can be hand or machine made. Usually found as wall hangings. The term should never be applied to canvas work embroidery.

Whitework generic term for embroidery worked in white thread on a white ground.

TEXTILES
Embroidery Stitches

Couching	the tying down of one thread by another. Very many varieties. Generally used to edge a piece of applied work such as figure on a banner.
Cross stitch	a cross either diagonal or vertical over 2 or 4 threads of canvas.
Gros point or half cross stitch	goes over 2 threads diagonally
Petit point or tent stitch	goes over one thread diagonally
Hem stitch	used to fasten the hems of altar linen. It may be worked by hand or, with bought altar linen, by machine.
Long and short stitch	forms a smooth surface. Used where shading is required.
Satin stitch	commonly found forming the monograms on altar linen
Split stitch	seldom found on 20th century work but in earlier work used for hands and faces.

Back

Couching

Blanket

Feather

Buttonhole

Herringbone

Chain

Satin

Chevron

Split

Cutwork

Darned netting

Drawn thread

Pattern darning

Quilting

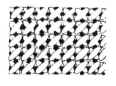

Cross

Eye

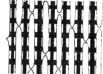

Florentine

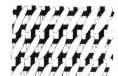

Gobelin

Hungarian

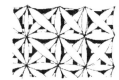

Italian

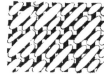

Mosaic

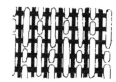

Parisian

Plait

Rice

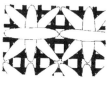

Smyrna

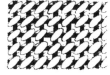

Tent or petit point

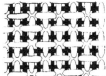

Upright cross

TEXTILES
Embroidery

Embroidered cope

of red silk damask decorated with applied crimson velvet, gold braid, green silk and canvas embroidered with gold thread, gold cord and silk in shades of green, yellow and brown: laid and couched work and metal spangles. The ground is powdered with fleurs-de-lys, sunbursts, stylized pineapples, scrolled foliage and the capital letter P surmounted by a crown.

On the false orphreys are ovals containing, at centre back, a Tudor rose and, down the sides, the initials S.P. (St Paul) alternating with the Sacred Monogram (IHS).

The round hood is trimmed with a fringe of gold thread and red silk and is attached to the cope by 5 silk and gold thread buttons. In the centre is an applied roundel with the Sacred Monogram IHS in Latin form, within a circle of rays; the same device appears on the morse (see page 44).

Most church lace is machine lace of the late 19th and early 20th centuries or 19th century hand-made lace applied to machine-made net. Earlier laces, however, were given to churches at the end of the 19th century and it is worth looking out for 17th century needle laces and 18th century bobbin laces. Machine-made lace was first introduced in the late 18th century.

Needlepoint lace

Developed from drawn-thread work, needlepoint lace is made with a single thread and needle, using embroidery stitches, dominated by buttonhole stitch.

Ecclesiastical robes and textiles are often adorned with **rose-point**, one of the many types of needlepoint, which consists of patterns worked in relief like sculptured work, forming strong and solid flowers and scrolls held in position by **brides** enriched with **picots**.

Pillow lace

Developed from knotted fringes and network, pillow lace is made with a multitude of threads wound upon bobbins stuck by pins into a pillow. The lace is created in a range of twists and plaits combining a varying number of threads, usually in or applied to a meshed ground. Where there is no **ground (fond or reseau)** the pattern is connected by **brides**.

Brides	bars or ties
Footing	straight edge or flouncing attached to material
Heading	scalloped or dentate free edge
Picots	small loops of twisted thread
Tallies	square or rectangular linking, characteristic of Buckinghamshire lace
Wheat ears	round or oval linking

TEXTILES
Veils and cloths

CLOTHS

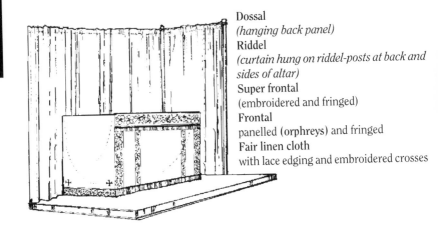

Dossal
(hanging back panel)
Riddel
(curtain hung on riddel-posts at back and sides of altar)
Super frontal
(embroidered and fringed)
Frontal
panelled (**orphreys**) and fringed
Fair linen cloth
with lace edging and embroidered crosses

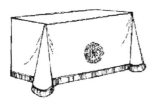

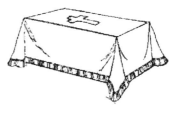

Laudian
(3 or 4 sided throw-over altar frontal with motif on one side only)

Funeral pall
(usually black, purple or white, with motif in centre or on all sides, sometimes corners are slit)

VEILS

Chalice veil
(silk square veil used to cover communion chalice when not in use, changing in colour according to the season).

Ciborium or pyx veil
(white linen circular veil with hole in centre under which Sacrament is reserved)

Monstrance veil
(made of white silk, without lining, with plain hemmed edges, nearly twice the height of monstrance)

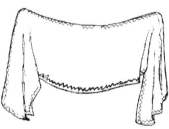

Humeral or offertory veil
(270 x 60cm)
(worn by priest when in procession or when moving the Sacrament; usually cream or white silk and lined)

Silk tabernacle veils
(in liturgical colours; divided in centre with hole for finial to protrude)

Aumbry veil   *covers door of aumbry; sometimes embroidered*
Lenten veil   *covers statues during Lent*

TEXTILES
Veils and cloths

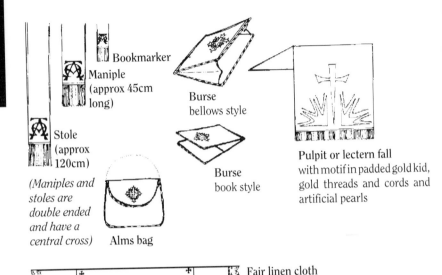

Bookmarker

Maniple
(approx 45cm
long)

Stole
(approx
120cm)

*(Maniples and
stoles are
double ended
and have a
central cross)*   Alms bag

Burse
bellows style

Burse
book style

Pulpit or lectern fall
with motif in padded gold kid,
gold threads and cords and
artificial pearls

Fair linen cloth
*(length and width of altar, usually with
lace or embroidered designs on edges)*

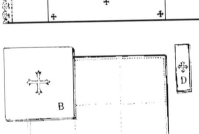

Communion linens
A. Corporal (50cm sq)
B. Communion veil, folded (45cm sq)
C. Palla (pl. pallae) also called pall board (15 cm sq)
D. Purificator (26cm sq)
E. Lavabo towel (Anglican 60 x 27)
    (Roman Catholic 50 x 40cm)

Communion cloth
*(small white linen napkin to catch
crumbs)*

Houselling cloth
*(white linen, the length of the
houselling bench (see p.175))*

Kneelers or **hassocks** protect worshippers from discomfort while kneeling. **Cushions** will be found on the altar, on the pulpit desk and the sanctuary chair. Long **padded runners** will be used at the communion rail for kneeling worshippers or on benches for the seated congregation.

Pair of pale blue velvet wedding kneelers
on each a white silk satin-stitch embroidered dove.

Kneeler with crossed keys embroidered in gold silk petit-point against a shaded grey wool gros-point field. Side edges covered completely with red wool cross stitch.

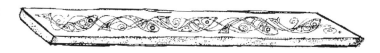

Emerald green velveteen bench runner
with a bold fish design and water effect. Applied and embroidered in gold and silver kid leathers, cords and metallic threads.

Red velvet altar cushion with corded edges and long tassels attached at the corners.

TEXTILES
Flags and Banners

Knight's Banner
square (90cm sq) bearing the owner's arms over the whole surface. Banners may also be rectangular. In size they will conform to protocol: Princes' or Dukes' banners should be 123 cm sq; the Sovereign's banner should be 150 cm sq. The banner commonly known as the **Royal Standard** is correctly The Sovereign's Banner

 Banner roll small square

Standard
either a long tapering flag split at the end, bearing the owner's device and motto (not arms or achievement) or an emblem on a staff.

Pennant or pennon
small pointed flag with two or more streamers, born at the lance head.
Gonfalon is similar but fixed to a bar.
Vexillum scarf attached to a staff .

Union Jack or Union Flag
national ensign of the United Kingdom, combining the national banners of England, Scotland and Ireland, which may be flown on land by any British subject.

Processional banner of the Mother's Union
straight hung through loops.
Figures of the Virgin and Child, in a combination of hand-worked appliqué and embroidery, against a pale blue ground. The name of the church at the top and the initials M U flanking the figures at the bottom. Blue and gold tasselled fringe.

Colour	infantry regimental flag
Colours	pair of infantry regimental flags
Other banners	might show St George; arms of the see or parish; the arms of a guild or society connected with the parish

Carpets will be found on floors or as coverings for tables and benches. A carpet over 100 years old is antique, over 50 years old is semi-antique and anything from 25 years ago can be regarded as old. The most famous carpets come from Persia and Afghanistan but, since the 15th century, Persian carpets have been copied by Spain, Poland (notable for European coats of arms), France (particularly tapestry carpets) and England, where they were copied in tent and cross stitch in the 16th and 17th centuries. A fine carpet is judged by the quality of the wool; the tightness of the weave (in general the more knots per square inch, the better the quality); and the clarity and beauty of the design. The first step is to distinguish between pile, flat woven and embroidered carpets, then to recognise the main oriental carpet producing areas, before attempting to identify the individual types within the areas, which will be of town, village, or tribal origin.

CARPET TYPES

Afghanistan	wine-red field with large stylised patterns
Caucasian	large geometric designs enclosed in multicoloured diagonal bands; dragons; soft rose colour relieved by dark blue or black; ghiordes knot.
Chinese	predominance of yellow; dragon, phoenix, lion, bat, cloud, swastika, pomegranate motifs.
Indian	cotton; light pastel colours; French, Persian or Chinese style designs.
Persian	repetitive all-over designs; central medallion, sometimes lobed or hung with festoons; decorated with pendants, lanterns and rectangular inscriptions; central motif often repeated at corners; gardens, hunting scenes & narratives (incl. Biblical) popular; sehna and ghiordes knots.
Turkish	small size; brilliant colours; borders with 7 ribbons decorated with flowers; geometric patterns; representations of Islamic mosque arch; no picture narratives; little green.
Turkoman	deep glowing red; geometric patterns with wavy brown outlines; repetitive octagons and hexagons divided in various ways, sometimes cross-wise into 4 parts arranged in parallel and perpendicular rows, known as **guls** (octagons) or **elephant's foot.**

PERSIAN SUB-TYPES

Feraghan	rusty background; palmettes and vegetation; Herati pattern; thin; green borders.
Hamadan	natural camelhair background; dark geometric medallions; tortoise motif; heavy; single knots.
Herat	dark blue or purple red background; closed rosettes in elongated leaves, ribbon-pattern, scroll or diamond; rosette with 8 points; green borders; very rich wool; rectangular shape; ghiordes or sehna knot.
Heriz	light background; well spaced geometric patterns.
Isfahan	bright background; symmetrical design; finely woven; round medallion with 8 or 16 points.
Kashan	small flowers filling centre and borders; soft silky wool; bouquets resembling peacock feathers.
Shiraz	tribal rugs; large medallions, stylised flowers, birds and animals.
Tabriz	plain background; large central medallion, repeated and quartered at corners; four seasons pattern; hunting scenes; ghiordes or sehna knot.

TEXTILES
Rugs and Carpets

KNOTS

Sehna knot
*(pile thread
twisted round
one warp)*

Ghiordes knot
*(pile thread
twisted around
two warps)*

Kelim
*(threads incorporated into
weaving so that rug can be
used on either side)*

Soumac
Weave

MAIN DESIGNS

Mihrab
(arch)

Medallion
*(classical town
design)*

Overall
(tribal design)

Geometric
*(village
design)*

BORDERS

Running dog

Crenellated

Recumbent S

T border

Tortoise

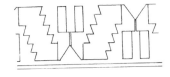

Wineglass

Writing
(in the borders) will be arabic, farsi, kufic, (or just decorative), telling the date, the maker,
or quoting a text from the Koran

CARPET MOTIFS

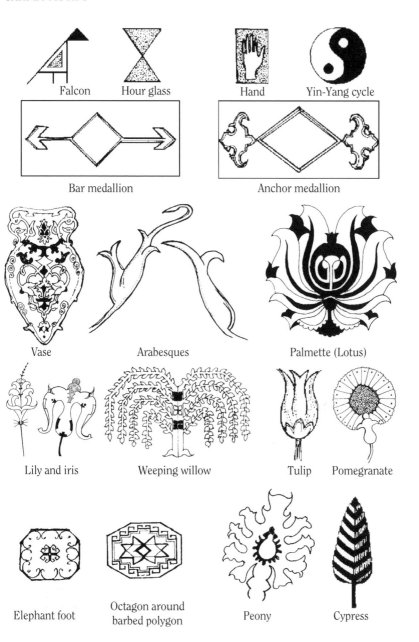

Falcon   Hour glass   Hand   Yin-Yang cycle

Bar medallion   Anchor medallion

Vase   Arabesques   Palmette (Lotus)

Lily and iris   Weeping willow   Tulip   Pomegranate

Elephant foot   Octagon around barbed polygon   Peony   Cypress

TEXTILES
Rugs and Carpets

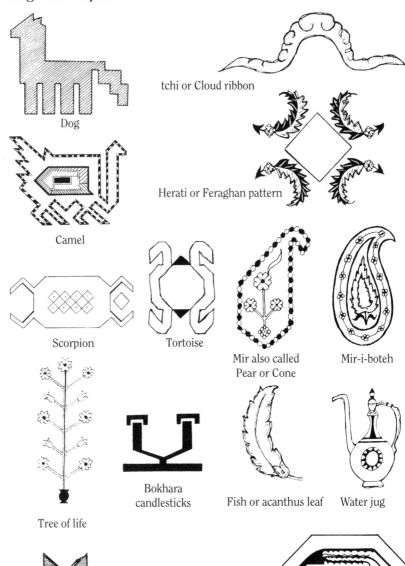

Dog

tchi or Cloud ribbon

Camel

Herati or Feraghan pattern

Scorpion

Tortoise

Mir also called
Pear or Cone

Mir-i-boteh

Tree of life

Bokhara
candlesticks

Fish or acanthus leaf

Water jug

Star of Solomon

Comb

Dragon and phoenix

WOOD
Terms

One of the most common materials employed in churches, wood is chiefly used for furniture, either fixed or free standing. Until about 1660 most furniture was made from oak. In the 17th century walnut and exotic fruitwood inlays became popular along with beech, pine and cane. The end of the 17th century saw the development of gesso and lacquering techniques, upholstery and yew became more common. In the mid-18th century, the apogee of English furniture making, mahogany and then satinwood, finally replaced oak in fine furniture.

WOODS

Ash	light brown with yellowish streaky grain
Beech	very pale brown, with satiny grain prone to woodworm, sometimes stained to resemble walnut and other timbers. Used for heavy country furniture.
Chestnut	almost indistinguishable from oak
Elm	brown and tough, often used for Windsor chair seats.
Mahogany	dark reddish brown, with slight grain. Not used before 1730.
Oak	heavy hardwood which darkens with age, distinctive figures from medullary rays.
Pine	yellow to red softwood. In use from 1660 and common in churches.
Teak	light or dark brown, heavy and durable. In use in 20th century.
Walnut	honey coloured (aged English wood) or darker red-brown (French and Italian) with tendency to woodworm. In use since 17th century
Yew	reddish to golden brown, very hard. Popular for country furniture.

CONSTRUCTION TECHNIQUES

Medieval furniture was held together by pegged mortise and tenon joints. Mouldings were cut in the solid and the corners turned with mason's mitres. From the mid-16th century, applied mouldings and mitred corners began to appear although pegged mortise and tenon joints were still used. From the mid-17th century joints need no longer be pegged. The dovetail joint, for carcase construction, was introduced c. 1660. Mouldings in 18th century furniture are generally applied and mitred.

Arris	sharp corner where two planes meet.
Dovetailed	fan-shaped projections interlaced to form tight flat joint.
Dowelled	round pins fitted into corresponding holes to make tight joint.
Framed construction	based on use of mortise and tenon joint.
Mitre	diagonal joint formed by 2 mouldings.
Mortise	slot to receive projection (tenon) on another piece of wood.
Tenon	projection protruded into mortise in another piece of wood.
Boarded construction	planks held in place by nails, or pegged with oak pins at the angles and strengthened with crosspieces.

WOOD
Terms

DECORATIVE TECHNIQUES

Applied	one piece of wood cut and applied to the surface of another.
Carving	wood cut or gouged out to leave shapes, which may be freestanding, in relief or pierced as tracery.
Chip carving	simple type of carved ornament used on wooden surfaces in the 13th, 14th and 15th centuries. The patterns, usually geometrical, were first set out with compasses and then chipped out, probably by the carpenter or joiner who made the chest. Chip carving persisted through the 16th and early 17th centuries.

Cock beading	small astragal or bead moulding applied to edges of drawer fronts.
Cross banding	strips of **veneer** at right angles to the rest of the surface.
Dado rail	wooden rail at height of chair backs on lower half of wall.
Feather banding	strips of **veneer** set diagonally to the rest of the surface.
Incising	cut or scratched into surface
Inlay	design cut from thin veneers of other woods and fitted into prepared cavities in the surface.
Marquetry	complicated inlay designs, first fashionable in Holland and France.
Mouldings	strips of wood of various shapes with names of architectural origin.
Parquetry	geometric patterns inlaid or glued together to form a composite veneer.
Pedestal	supporting base for statue, object etc. rising to height of dado.
Skirting	horizontal base board around bottom of wall.
Stringing	inlay of thin lines of wood or bone.
Veneer	thin sheet of richly **figured** *(grained)* wood, ivory or tortoiseshell glued to the surface of another material (see **cross banding** and **feather banding**).

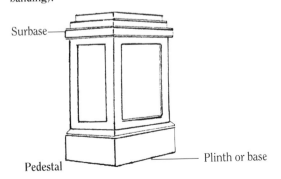

Surbase

Pedestal

Plinth or base

Baldacchino
(canopy over altar, throne or doorway).

Bracket
(decorative or functional support for object).

Console
(any bracket or corbel of scrolled form).

Console
(desk-like frame of organ, containing keyboards, stops etc.).

Bracket

pierced and pinnacled in the form of a flying buttress.

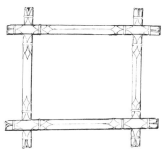

Console mirror
(mirror supported by bracket against wall).

Oxford frame
(type of frame for pictures and texts, with the horizontal and vertical members forming a cross at each corner. Crossed ends of this type were used on hymn boards in churches in the 1830s).

Console table
(table supported by bracket against wall).

WOOD

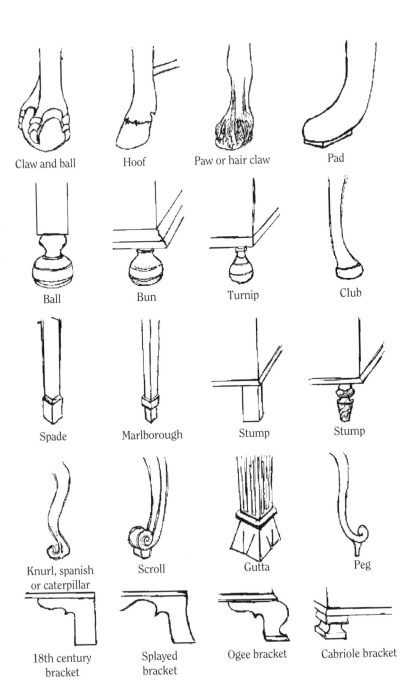

Claw and ball   Hoof   Paw or hair claw   Pad

Ball   Bun   Turnip   Club

Spade   Marlborough   Stump   Stump

Knurl, spanish or caterpillar   Scroll   Gutta   Peg

18th century bracket   Splayed bracket   Ogee bracket   Cabriole bracket

WOOD

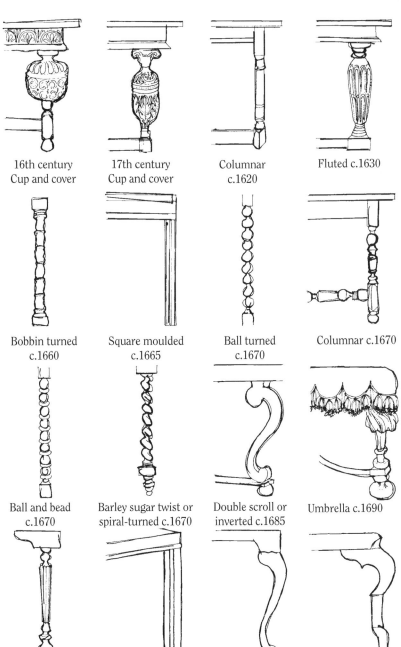

16th century
Cup and cover

17th century
Cup and cover

Columnar
c.1620

Fluted c.1630

Bobbin turned
c.1660

Square moulded
c.1665

Ball turned
c.1670

Columnar c.1670

Ball and bead
c.1670

Barley sugar twist or
spiral-turned c.1670

Double scroll or
inverted c.1685

Umbrella c.1690

Turned tapered
c.1690

Square chamfered
(inside) from 1740

18th century
Cabriole

18th century
Broken cabriole

WOOD
Legs

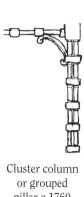

Cluster column
or grouped
pillar c.1760

Carved or applied
fret c.1765

Square tapered
c.1775

18th century
Hipped cabriole

Fluted vase stem
Late 17th century

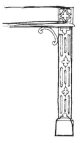

Pierced fret
c.1790

Reeded columnar
c.1803

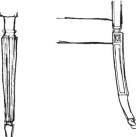

Sabre c.1815

Vase-shaped, slab
standard or trestle

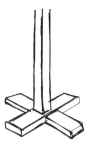

Cruciform

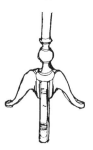

Tripod foot
on stem

Splayed, split and
wedged through seat

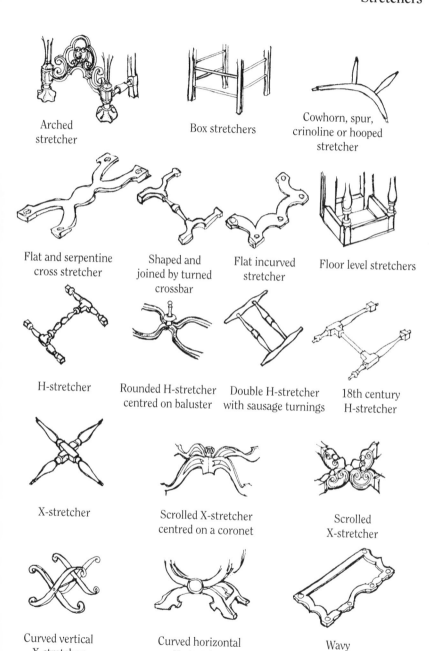

Arched stretcher

Box stretchers

Cowhorn, spur, crinoline or hooped stretcher

Flat and serpentine cross stretcher

Shaped and joined by turned crossbar

Flat incurved stretcher

Floor level stretchers

H-stretcher

Rounded H-stretcher centred on baluster

Double H-stretcher with sausage turnings

18th century H-stretcher

X-stretcher

Scrolled X-stretcher centred on a coronet

Scrolled X-stretcher

Curved vertical X-stretcher

Curved horizontal X-stretcher

Wavy

WOOD

WOOD
Panels

Most panels are bevelled or rebated to fit into a groove in the surrounding framework. Mouldings may be added (**bed** moulding or **bolection** moulding) to conceal the junction of the panel with the framework. **Wainscoating** is the term generally used for wood panelling on walls up to **dado** height.

Coffered panels have a deeply sunk surface below the level of the framework, differing from **sunk panels** which are shallower.

Styles of panelling have been copied in different periods.

15th century
Gothic *(pierced)*

15th and 16th centuries
Gothic *(pierced)*

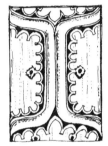

Early 16th century
Parchment

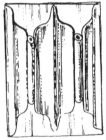

Early 16th century
Linenfold

Romayne
c.1530-1550

Mid 16th century
Renaissance

From 18th century
Fielded *(raised)*

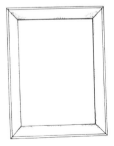

From 18th century
Coffered

19th and 20th centuries
Applied Gothic tracery

ALTAR AND COMMUNION RAILS

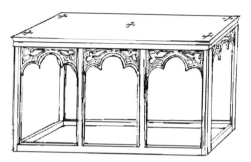

19th or 20th century purpose built Altar

Rectangular frame with plain overhanging Altar-top incised with five Consecration crosses, set on a projecting cornice.

Front divided into three bays, back open, sides and each bay of the front contain, at the top, pierced tracery panels with two cusps below the arch and spandrel panels following the shape of the top of the bays. Most of the members of the framework, which stands on a base of rails are chamfered on the outside.

Remember to record the line of the joints. Similar constructions, usually hidden by the frontal, often have the fronts and sides panelled with applied Gothic tracery, the back being left open.

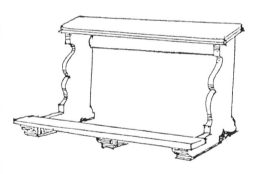

Communion rail

Sloped capping with moulded edges raised on solid end-supports shaped and cut with ogee sections along one side: the supports are braced by a medial top rail and rest on base runners of ogee design bearing a kneeling board which has been set on oak blocks to allow a restful posture, the joints are pegged.

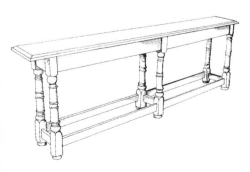

Houselling benches

Long wooden stools with a flat table/stool top. Used as communion rails, sometimes with a kneeler along one of the long sides. Can be used with a **Houselling cloth** draped across the top. Height approx. 60cm.

WOOD
Furniture

BENCHES, PEWS AND CONFESSIONALS

Benches are seats with supports whereas pews are enclosed or elevated seating. The backs of benches usually have open rails or panels and will often have **bookrests** fitted to them for the use of the occupants of the bench behind. If the bookrests have flat surfaces they may date from before the Reformation. Post-Reformation bookrests are usually sloping. Each section of benches will probably include a bench front or desk. Bench ends are often decorated with carvings and finials usually called **poppyheads**.

Pews have panels, doors and benches and may be raised above the floor or canopied or furnished and heated. Some are painted or carved with the names or coats of arms of families. The most popular material was oak until the 19th century when pine examples also appeared.

Stalls are individual or multiple seats placed against or sometimes **returned** *(at right angles)* against a wall or screen. Some have tabernacled canopies, or traceried backs and cornices and nearly all have shaped side-panelling sometimes with carved or applied elbows. The stall fronts (or **desks**) may be traceried and have poppyheads. Tip-up seats known as **misericords,** may be ornately carved on the underside. Subsidiary carvings on either side of the main projection are known as **supporters.**

Bench with close boarded back, moulded top rail and curved ends to the seat.
Carved rectangular bench-end.
Unicorn below an arch supporting a pomegranate with branches flowing from top of stem to top of arch.
Plain gouged blind arcade below.

Bench front with integral kneeler and level bookrest.
Rectangular arch-topped end with lively 16th century carving incorporating 2 quatrefoils below a Pelican in her Piety and a foliated poppyhead.
Colonnade of trefoil headed arches between top and bottom rails, with pierced triangular spandrels.

Open backed bench with two rails and one shaped end with simple, moulded edging the other end flush with wall.

176

WOOD

Stalls of 4 bays with a Canopy formed of a cusped ogee arch over each stall, decorated with flame-like crockets and fleur-de-lys finials and supported by moulded shafts from the shoulder rail.
Moulded scrolled elbows.
Misericords carved on the underside with a Green Man.

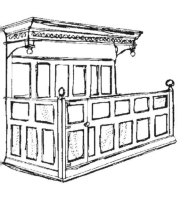

Early 17th century Box Pews

18th century Box Pews

WOOD
Furniture

CONFESSIONAL

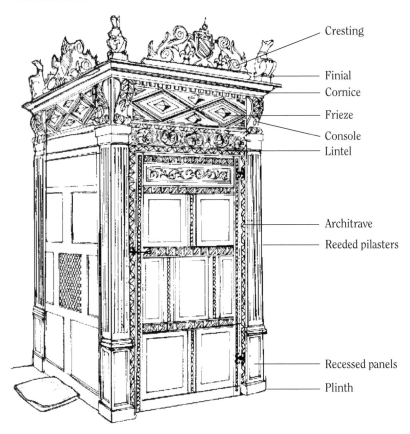

Cresting

Finial
Cornice

Frieze

Console
Lintel

Architrave
Reeded pilasters

Recessed panels

Plinth

Confessional

(possibly adapted from an Elizabethan internal porch) of square frame and panel construction of armoire style, with reeded pilasters on pedestals with recessed panels. The rails of the door carved with a geometric lined motif, the muntins and stiles with guilloche, the architrave with irregular chevrons, the fielded panels plain except for the horizontal top panel which bears a foliated scroll carving tied at the centre. There is large palmette carving on the lintel and the console brackets supporting the entablature are carved with leaves, the frieze is enriched with mitred lozenge moulding surmounted by dentil moulding, the latter omitted on the sides of the pew.

The sides do not have any enrichment below the frieze and consoles: on one side is a metal grille set in a panel at eye-level for someone kneeling.

Above the moulded cornice are dog-like corner finials, squatting on square plinths and holding shields between their paws; crestings of coats-of-arms amidst floriated scrolls and fleurs-de-lys are set between them.

BOXES

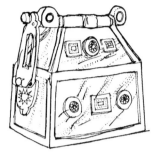

Feretory
(container for saint's relics)
Metal rod across the gabled top
secures the hasp and has eyelets for
attaching priest's neck cord.
Pierced round and rectangular
apertures in roof and sides.

16th century oak alms box
Rectangular with domed lid bound
with iron straps and decorated with
enamelled tracery.

17th century oak alms box
Rectangular with carved date
and inscription on front:
1684/
REMEMBER/
THE PORE
in contemporary lettering,
and supported by a bracket
decorated with leaves.

17th century poor box
Oak post, the top hollowed to form
a box.
Lid with coin slot has 3 iron straps
hinged at front and secured to post
by padlocks.
Simple applied moulding runs
around 3 sides of the post.

WOOD
Furniture

17th century desk-type oak Bible Box
Flat top, sloping flap with butterfly hinges.
Typical Lake District style interlace carving
on the front flanking a keyplate above the date
1675.
Neatly moulded edges
Document drawers *(upright drawers)* within.

17th century rectangular Bible Box
with original lock and hasp.
2 large lunettes carved on front enclosing
stylised leaf decoration and similar motifs in
spandrels.

20th century Book of Remembrance stand
Desk top with glazed viewing panel, supported
on a metal frame of a pair of standards united
by 2 stretchers and fixed to the rear base of the
desk.
The feet curving forward to take balance.

20th century Book of Remembrance stand
in Gothic style.
Table style box with glazed top above carved
frieze of running vine leaf ornament
Rectangular panels of reticulated tracery
running between legs on all 4 sides
immediately below frieze and with blank shield
at centre front.
Shelf unites the 4 legs of square section.

CHESTS

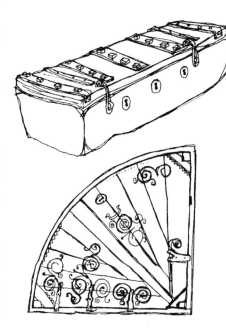

Medieval dugout chest
Hollowed log with solid slab lid, strengthened by 5 iron bands and strap hinges, provision for 3 locks and 2 padlock loops which were probably later additions.

13th century cope chest
Quadrant shaped with frame of stout posts at corners into which rails are tenoned.
Lid in 2 halves with ornate scrolled and foliated iron hinges and decoration.
Panels of sides nailed into rebates in frame.

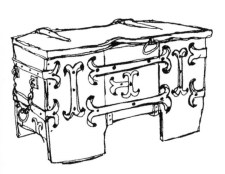

Early 14th century chest
Front and back tenoned into wide stiles extended to provide legs.
Iron straps, binding the chest with bifurcated decorative ends.
Chains with rings suspended from them, fixed to the sides.

Flanders chest 1550 to 1600
Front of 2 wide vertical stiles and 2 wide horizontal planks.
Traces of painted decoration in fantastic bestiary scenes on the stiles.
Between the stiles the front is decorated with curvilinear blind tracery.

WOOD
Furniture

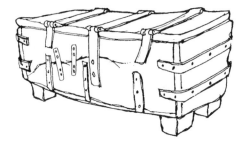

14th to 16th century chest
Massive planks pegged into corner posts of square section raising chest from floor strengthened by angled iron straps and flat straps (which strengthen the breaks in the timber). Strap hinges continuing across top hinged to hasps and locks.

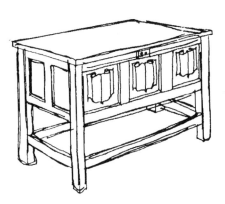

16th century counter
Chest with long legs about table height
Top sometimes scored.

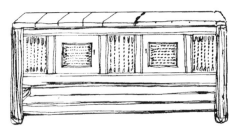

Early 17th hutch chest
Frame and panel construction with 5 panels at front and 2 at the sides decorated with simple linenfold. Two of the front panels were originally doors but are now secured to the frame.
Top of chest sawn and hinged for access.
2 stretchers run across the length of the chest at floor level.

WOOD

WOOD
Furniture

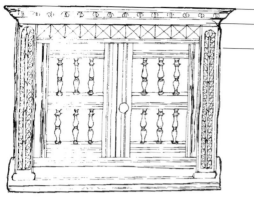

Cornice
Frieze

Pilaster strips

Early 17th century dole cupboard
Stamped enrichment on cornice
Geometric inlay on frieze.
2 doors, each with 6 turned spindles in 2 stages.
Pilaster strips carved with stiff leaves.

17th century mule chest
(shallow type of panelled chest with drawers in lower part)

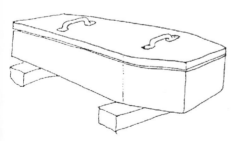

18th century mortsafe
(earlier mortsafes usually lidless and of stone)

Late 18th century mahogany chest of drawers
Serpentine-fronted chest with oversailing top and cross-banded canted corners, 3 long drawers with cockbeading, swan-necked Rococo brass handles and C-scrolled escutcheons.
A slide above the top drawer.
Splayed feet with bow-shaped apron on front and sides.

WOOD
Furniture

Mid-19th century walnut Davenport
Scrolled front uprights supporting scrolled flap, 4 drawers on left side and cupboard door concealing 3 drawers on other side.
Ink drawer on left.
Bun feet.
Use of term 'Davenport' sufficient to describe the style.

19th century military chest
With brass corners and sunken handles, usually mahogany (upper stage sometimes a secretaire).

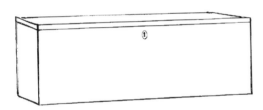

19th and 20th century frontal chest
Hinged top-opening to enable frontals to be hung on rods.
105cm x 300cm x 30cm
Usually of softwood.

19th and 20th century linen and vestment press
Usually of softwood.

CHAIRS

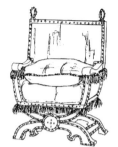

Chair of state c.1600
Armchair of horizontal X-frame construction, closely covered in crimson velvet, trimmed with fringed gold gallon and garnished with gilt-headed nails and fitted with down stuffed cushion covered en suite.

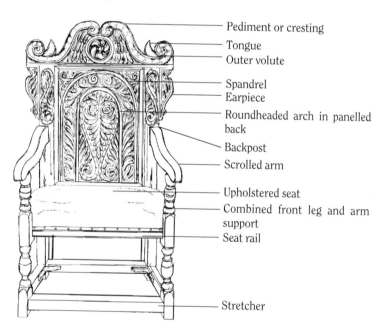

Pediment or cresting
Tongue
Outer volute
Spandrel
Earpiece
Roundheaded arch in panelled back
Backpost
Scrolled arm
Upholstered seat
Combined front leg and arm support
Seat rail
Stretcher

Yorkshire chair 1625-1650
Panel back construction, panel carved with roundheaded arch decorated with scrolled foliage.
Scrolled pediment with tongues protruding beside outer volutes carved with foliage and central roundel.
Carving similar to that on the back, on earpieces and back-posts above scrolled arms.
Turned front uprights of baluster form sectioned by blocked joints.
Seat upholstered in red figured velvet with various reinforcements.
Plain renewed stretchers.
In chairs of this type, the backs are sometimes raked, seats splayed, stretchers and front uprights vary in form.

WOOD
Furniture

Glastonbury chair c.1630

Chair with panel back and X-shaped legs joined by crossbar. Shaped arms from seat to back, both held by wooden pins.

The only description required, beyond 'Glastonbury', is the rake of the back, shape of the arms and decoration, which may be on both the inside and rear of the back and arms, the wood, measurements and date.

Oak Armchair of Box form Cambridgeshire c.1530

Square back, surmounted at either end by the figure of a crouching lion, with an oblong panel of finely carved Renaissance design consisting of male and female terminal figures supporting a trophy of arms, their tails ending in scrolls. Below are 2 rectangular linenfold panels.

Flat arms enclose plain panels.

Lower part of the back is fitted behind with a cupboard door.

2 linenfold panels in front of the box of simpler design than those on the back.

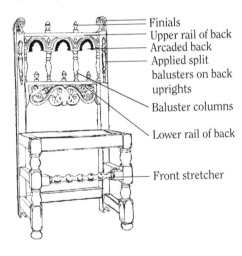

— Finials
— Upper rail of back
— Arcaded back
— Applied split balusters on back uprights
— Baluster columns
— Lower rail of back

— Front stretcher

Mid-17th century Yorkshire or Derbyshire chair

Arcaded back, the upper rail having three arches with carved and incised decoration and cusping supported by two baluster columns resting on a lower rail with leafy scrolls; the upper rail surmounted by two, and the lower by three knob finials. The back uprights have crozier-shaped finials and applied split baluster ornaments. Spirally turned front stretcher, the rest plain. Front legs have new feet: back legs slotted for castors. Seat sunk for a squab cushion.

Early 17th century Jacobean oak settle
Top rail of back treated with lunettes
Lozenge carving in 4-panelled back.

Lancashire panel back chair c.1660
Flat pyramidal caps to backposts.
Lunette cresting carved with a tulip amidst sprawling foliage above similar carving with a dog-rose on rectangular panel.
Opening below panel.
Moulded seat rails.
Turned front legs.
Bobbin-turned front rail stretcher.

Walnut armchair c.1670
The cresting of the back and of the rail joining the front cabriole legs is elaborately carved in openwork with putti crowning a female figure, flanked by putti blowing trumpets.
Spiral uprights with crowned female head finials.
Lion couchant on each armrest.
Sides of the back adorned with openwork carvings of putti amidst vines and roses growing from baskets.
Original canework back; seat (formerly caned) upholstered in green velvet.

WOOD

WOOD
Furniture

Beech Chair c.1690
Tall back with moulded arched cresting rail, with ears, and straight back rail enclosing 5 vertical moulded spars.
Front seat rail has veneered and shaped apron, hidden by fringe of red Victorian plush covering the slightly tapered seat.
Turned front legs with ball feet, united by a turned front stretcher rail.
Turned H-stretchers unite all 4 legs, the back legs being slightly splayed.
Mouldings where back uprights join cresting rail have been carefully mitred at each corner.

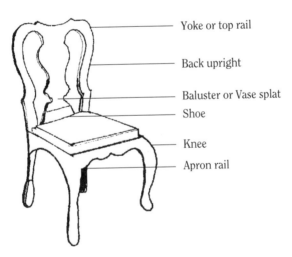

- Yoke or top rail
- Back upright
- Baluster or Vase splat
- Shoe
- Knee
- Apron rail

Early 18th century Side Chair
Splat back with serpentine top rail, cabriole front legs with pad feet, wavy apron rail and no underframing. Drop-in tapestry covered seat.

Mid 19th century Hall Chair
Oval back supported on C scrolls of X-frame construction.

The rococo scrolls of the back and the tied X are ornamented with carved acanthus decoration.

Seat has heavily fluted seat rails.

WOOD

19th and 20th century church chair
Beech frame and elm or rush seat.

Top rail usually shaped *(yoked in illustration)*

Middle rails often bowed.

Elm seats are usually saddle shaped.

Book pocket between backposts.

Box stretchers with attached shelf for kneeler.

WOOD
Furniture

COUNTRY STYLE CHAIRS

Windsor chairs
The most popular country chair design of the 19th century is very distinctive and often found in churches. Windsor chairs come in many shapes but usually have elm seats, beech spindles (struts, stays or rods), beech legs and stretchers, and ash bowed parts.
The legs and supports are pegged into the seat; the legs are splayed. In some examples, two stays form a brace from the top of the back to a bobtail projecting from the rear of the seat. A horizontal hoop forms a semi-circle across the back and along to the front as arm supports. Every variant of style has a name, for example, if the hoop is missing and the back bowed, the chair is a **Single-bowed** Windsor. Most Windsor chairs were made in Buckinghamshire.

Hoopback Windsor

Gothic hoopback Windsor

Lowback Windsor

Tablet top Windsor

Comb back Windsor

Bow back Windsor

Bow

Splat (wheelback)

Stays

Bobtail (hidden)

Front upright

Saddle seat

Spur stretcher

18th century Yew
Gothic Windsor armchair
Arch bow
Ash saddle seat
Cabriole legs
Club feet
Crinoline (spur) stretcher and turned back
supports

19th century
Mendlesham Windsor armchair
Low back with double crest rail of square
section infilled with 3 turned balls.
Vase-shaped splat flanked by 3 sticks.
Flat outward curving arms extending beyond
sloping supports.
Saddle seat, splayed legs and H-stretcher.

Smoker's Bow
Windsor c.1860
Double H-stretcher

Lath back
Windsor

High back
Ladderback

WOOD
Furniture

CHAIRBACKS

Queen Anne

Prince of
Wales feather

Fiddle

Shield

Ladder

Square

Lyre

Riband

Gothic

Oval
Late
18th century

Balloon
19th century

Gothic
19th century

Shouldered balloon
19th century

Elizabethan
19th century

Spoon hall seat
19th century

WOOD
Furniture

DOORS

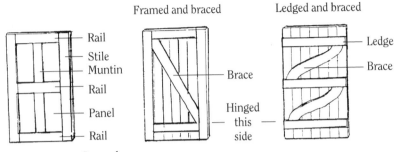

Framed and braced

Ledged and braced

Rail
Stile
Muntin
Rail
Panel
Rail

Brace

Hinged
this
side

Ledge
Brace

Saxon door
ledged vertical boards backed by horizontal boards

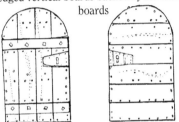

Saxon doors were stout defences made of thick oak boards placed vertically on the outside and horizontal ly inside. Showing toolmarks and fastened together by long wrought-iron nails with ornamental heads, driven through the door and clenched on the inside. Ledges were always confined to the back or inside of the door.

Norman door with alternating horizontal hinges with double scrolled bifurcated terminals

In the 12th century, although construction techniques were similar, doors were often decorated by the smith with wrought-iron hinges, locks, handles and knockers. The hinges usually have bifurcated ends and stamped work of contemporary design.

The smith declined in prominence in the 14th century and decoration on doors came into the realm of the carpenter. Locks and hinges were plainer. Besides mouldings or cover beads to cover the joints, tracery was either carved into the woodwork or applied with glue and nails.

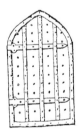

14th century door   14th century door

In the late 17th century the smith's craft enjoyed a slight revival and decorated hinges reappeared. The majority of churches have 19th century doors, often exact copies of earlier Norman doors but the decoration on the later doors tends to be more precise.

WOOD

FONT COVERS

In the medieval period, wooden font covers (often highly decorative) were fitted to fonts to protect the holy water. Medieval font covers were copied in the 19th century as part of the Gothic Revival movement. Octagonal shapes, which had a mystical connotation, were frequently used in Gothic work.

Crown font cover

Simple octagonal flat cover moulded at the edge, supporting 8 ogee scrolls rising from the angles and meeting at the head of a central baluster-shaped post, just below the bulb final. The volute of each scroll is carved with a rosette on both sides.

Pointed Cone font cover

Lightly moulded octagonal base with moulded ribs, enclosing flat panels. Each rib decorated with 3 crockets and rising from each of the 8 angles to the neck, surmounted by a four-tier finial.

Font cover

Pinnacled and spired in 3 stages incorporating telescopic device for lifting by font crane.

Highest stage: lofty crocketed pinnacle with gables at base and finial top, supported on five slender annulated columns.

Middle stage: cruciform in plan, with four slender annulated compound columns at centre, flanked by eight slender annulated columns in pairs supporting a roof with four projecting crocketed gables.

Lowest stage: square in plan; at each angle flying diagonal buttresses culminating in crocketed pinnacles; at each side a panel carved with two foliage filled quatrefoils below, and above, an open pointed arch with bead moulding on the extrados and enclosing geometrical tracery, supported on slender central annulated columns; the crown of the arch breaking into a crocketed gable with a pierced trefoil in its upper angle. Inside, painted figures of Christ kneeling and John the Baptist standing.

Base with a band of moulding formed from a geometrical pattern of mostly circular indentations, and with a band of imbricated decoration inclined inwards.

WOOD
Furniture

PULPITS AND DESKS

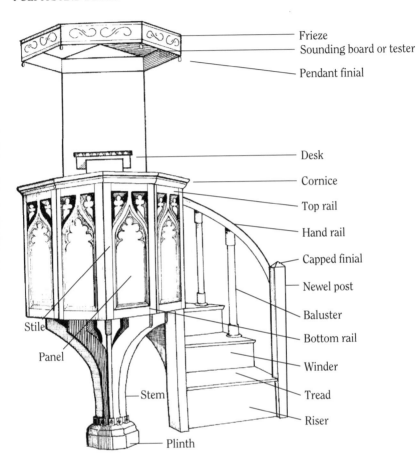

Frieze
Sounding board or tester
Pendant finial
Desk
Cornice
Top rail
Hand rail
Capped finial
Newel post
Baluster
Bottom rail
Stile
Panel
Winder
Stem
Tread
Riser
Plinth

15th century oak pulpit
Octagonal drum, the panels on each of the 6 visible facets richly carved with blind tracery, consisting of cinquefoil ogee arches, crocketed top edge, but no finials.
The spandrels have trefoil tracery flanking the ogee arches.
The two arches are subdivided by a centre stile.
Desk made from 15th or 16th century oak with carved edges.
19th century stem with attached brackets on octagonal plinth.
19th century hexagonal sounding board with pendant finials at each angle and frieze of scrolled carving.
19th century stairway of 4 threads on S side.
Plain rectangular newel post with pyramidal capped finial, grooved hand rail and plain balusters.

WOOD
Furniture

18th century 3-decker pulpit

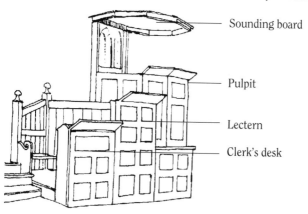

— Sounding board

— Pulpit

— Lectern

— Clerk's desk

19th century oak lectern *(see METAL: Lecterns)*
Desk supported on solid cruciform brackets with shaped and bevelled edges, each bracket pierced in the centre with a quatrefoil.
Stem of clustered shafts with annulets attached to rectangular central shaft.
Cruciform base with plain sill and similar brackets to those above.

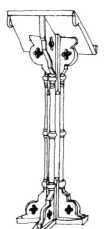

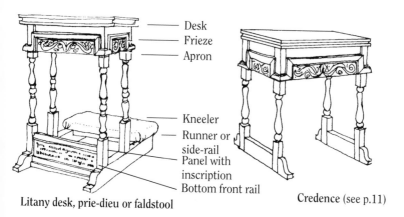

— Desk
— Frieze
— Apron

— Kneeler
— Runner or side-rail
— Panel with inscription
— Bottom front rail

Litany desk, prie-dieu or faldstool

Credence (see p.11)

WOOD

WOOD
Furniture

RAILS

Moulded oak top rail
Wrought-iron cylindrical supports (or standards) with spiral-twist centre sections between knots, and ivy decorated brackets splaying either side of upper two-thirds: octagonal buttressed bases.
Bottom oak sill forms integral kneeler.

Moulded top rail with incised lunettes on frieze.
Pillar-turned balusters between sturdier standards of the same shape which have cup and cover finials.
Grooved and domed bottom rail tenoned into bases of standards, the balusters resting on the rail.

17th or 18th century Laudian *(enclosing altar)* **communion rail**

Gallery (or tribune) with Balustrade consisting of groups of five turned balusters separated by fluted stiles. Festooned frieze above lower cornice.

SCREENS

Screens, particularly those which divided the chancel from the centre of the church, were an essential part of medieval religious practice. The congregational principles of the Reformation led to the wholesale destruction of chancel screens which were not generally reintroduced until the 19th century. Screens or **parcloses** were also used, to separate side chapels and other areas of the church.

On rood screens, the Rood figures are usually placed centrally with the cross on a tall pedestal and the flanking figures on small pedestals. Original groups are very rare, though a few survive in Wales, and most date from the religious revival of the 1840's. Many were polychromed and a torch or magnifying glass often reveals traces of original colour in the corners and recesses. Where the chancel arch was boarded in above the rood screen, the resultant tympanum was sometimes painted with a Doom scene showing the division of souls into Heaven or Hell.

Screens are usually divided into a series of bays with an opening which may or may not be gated. The outer bays are generally panelled at the base and open, except for the posts, between the **transom** *(centre)* rail and the **head** *(top)* rail. The heads of the **lights** *(openings)* usually have pierced carved tracery.

Bressumer beam	horizontal beam supporting main superstructure.
Ceilure	section of roof directly above rood screen, sometimes richly decorated as canopy to the rood.
Chancel screen	dividing chancel from nave.
Chantry screen	dividing tomb from chancel or nave.
Parclose screen	separating chapel from body of church.
Quire screen or pulpitum	dividing eastern section of cruciform church from body of church (opposite rood screen).
Rood beam	beam spanning chancel arch supporting **rood** *(Christ on the Cross).*
Rood screen	screen incorporating Christ on the Cross invariably flanked by figures of Mary (right) and St John (left).
Roodloft	space above vaulted or coved rood screen which supports gallery fronts at east and west sides.
Tower screen	separating tower from nave.

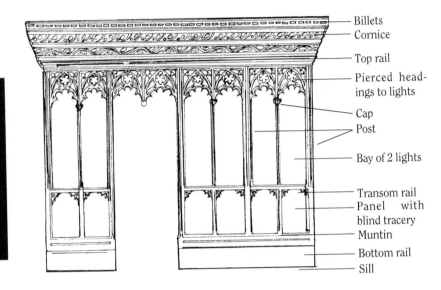

Billets
Cornice
Top rail
Pierced head-
ings to lights
Cap
Post
Bay of 2 lights
Transom rail
Panel with
blind tracery
Muntin
Bottom rail
Sill

Screen

of 4 bays, the opening in 2nd bay from N end.

Heavy overhanging cornice crested with billet moulding, below which are moulded fillets enclosing two bands of frieze, the upper one carved with pellets and gadrooning, the lower with an undulating vine; below are more bands of stepped moulding resting on the top rail.

Each bay contains two lights, between slender reeded posts with cinqefoil heads and pierced tracery beneath pointed arches with trefoil piercing in the spandrels of the upper arches.

The lower stage, either side of the passageway, has blind cinquefoil headed arches applied to the fielded panels.

All frame members have applied mouldings.

The screen stands on a deep and solid plinth with chamfered top edge.

WOOD

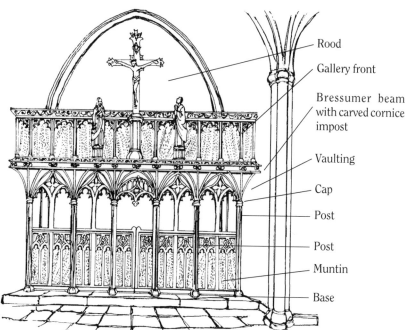

Rood

Gallery front

Bressumer beam
with carved cornice
impost

Vaulting

Cap

Post

Post

Muntin

Base

WOOD

Vaulted rood screen
of 5 bays, the centre bay having a pair of doors, gallery front on the west side.
Central cross on tall octagonal pedestal with cap and base and carved ornamental
terminals to the arms and pierced tracery at the central intersection. The label with
INRI appears above the head of the traditionally carved Christus, figures of the Blessed
Virgin Mary and St. John flank the Crucifix, both have their hands clasped in prayer,
their heads and shoulders protruding above the panelling, stand on reeded pedestals.
The rood beam is carved with 2 rows of carved ornament (flowing foliage over deep
hollow paterae) spaced over each post and arch.
Reeded posts carry the ribbed vaulting beneath the loft which is panelled, with a blind
cinquefoil headed arch in each of the 10 full and 2 half panels, surmounted by a cornice
of carved running ornament.
Above the transom rail there are 5 bays, each with a two-light cinquefoil headed
opening united with a central quatrefoil beneath a pointed arch. Beneath the transom
rail the panels are carved with blind trefoil headed arcading. The centre bay is wider
than side bays with a pair of doors to the height of the transom rail, each with full
panels decorated as side bays, but with posts which meet and rise above the transom
rail to form a finial on each door.

Furniture

STOOLS

Chairs developed from more simple stool shapes but never completely supplanted stools. Early inventories distinguish between highstools, lowstools, foot stools and elbow *(arm)* or back *(side)* chairs. The medieval backstool, in use until the late 18th century, is the hybrid with most in common with stools and chairs.

Backstool c.1600

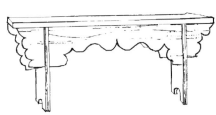

Oak form c.1520 of plank construction Apron, extending beyond solid supports to ends of seat, is of ogee shape with rounded ends.
Supports have moulded edges and arched openings below.

Joined stool from 1550
4 turned legs splayed outwards united by a rail beneath the seat linked by floor level stretchers.
(19th century coffin stools are similar but with longer legs)

Early 17th century folding X-type faldstool

Baroque stool with Braganza feet c. 1690
Arched and scrolled central stretcher, 2 turned side stretchers with block central section.

TABLES

14th to 16th century oak trestle table
Plank top supported by trestles with ogee opening at base.
Pair of central stretchers with protruding tenons secured by wooden wedges.

Elizabethan oak drawleaf table c.1600
Moulded frieze with deeply carved diagonal gadrooning.
4 bulbous legs with cups carved with acanthus and gadrooned covers.
Rectangular section floor-level stretchers.
Gadrooning often referred to as nulling

Jacobean oak table c.1640
Top formed of 3 planks with apron, 6 thin tapered turned legs joined by square section stretchers.

17th century country oak side table
Inlaid banding of fruit wood let into solid oak around top and drawer.
Wide apron rail of William and Mary style with cockbeading around the edge.
Neatly turned legs of baluster shape.
Joints pegged
Barley twist H-stretchers.

WOOD
Furniture

Oak side table c.1670
Frame of halved hexagonal shape with circular top folded in centre.
Gate at rear with square section stretcher
6 turned baluster legs.
Halved hexagonal bottom board.

Stuart dresser
c.1680

Gate-leg table
c.1730

D-end table
c.1780

Pembroke table
c.1800

Sofa table
c.1820

20th century credence (see p. 11)
Moulded top-rail stretcher between plain pillar trestles with chamfered corners, to which is attached an ogee shaped apron carved with cursive lilies.
Plain moulded domed bottom stretcher.

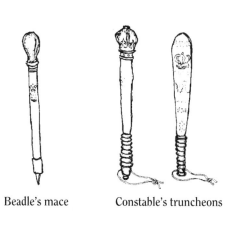

Beadle's mace   Constable's truncheons

Collection plate

Collection ladles

OBJECTS

The clock in the tower (with or without an external dial) is known as a **turret** or **tower clock**. Most dioceses have a Clocks Adviser who may be contacted through the Secretary of the Diocesan Advisory Committee. Vestries may contain a variety of domestic clocks, which may be broadly divided into two classes, **wall-hanging** and **free standing**.

Wall Hanging
The commonest wall clock is the **dial clock**, spring driven and contained in a circular wooden case, occasionally with a downward extension to accommodate a longer pendulum. **Tavern** or **Act of Parliament** clocks have a long trunk section to accomodate weights and a long pendulum. **Lantern** or **hood clocks** may occasionally be found.

Free Standing
Of free-standing clocks the most usual are **mantel** or **bracket clocks** which are spring driven and stand upon a mantelpiece, or other horizontal surface. **Longcase** or **grandfather clocks** are less likely to be found, these are weight driven and stand on the floor.

In addition, some clocks are built into galleries or other parts of the structure. The maker's name will usually give a clue to the date but only if features of the clock and case support his dates. Baillie's and Loomes's books are useful *(see FURTHER READING)*, but there are still omissions and as different generations of a family often had the same christian names, confusion can occur.

Bob	weight at end of pendulum.
Dial	clock face.
Fret	pierced brass decoration on lantern clocks or sound aperture on later clocks.
Fusée	grooved cone to equalise power of mainspring.
Hood	top section of longcase clock which generally lifts or slides off.
Lenticle	glass let into the door of a longcase clock to allow motion of bob to be seen; less common by c. 1710.
Movement	working parts of clock.
Weights	cylindrical lead, cast iron or brass cased weights hung from chains or other lines.

Hooded
clock
with
weights
c.1745

Lantern
clock
with
weights
c.1680

Tavern or Act of
Parliament clock
late 18th century
Weight-driven
and unglazed

CLOCKS
Types

WALL HANGING CLOCKS
Dial Clocks
Cases are ebonised or of common furniture woods, while some early 19th century ones have brass or mother of pearl inlay. Later examples of German or American clocks have fancy inlay bandings and usually have a downward extension with a glazed door showing the pendulum. Clocks with this extension are known as **drop dial clocks**.

Dials: Early ones may be of silvered brass and some painted wooden specimens survive. The vast majority are made of painted iron, some convex but most flat. German and American clocks have dials of painted zinc.

Movements: English movements have a fusée and only a few strike. German and American clocks have open springs, no fusées and usually strike.

FREE STANDING CLOCKS
Longcase Clocks
Cases are made of the same woods and have the same designs and mouldings as furniture, but mahogany is rare before 1750. In general later ones are taller and broader than early examples, but many cottage clocks follow smaller, simpler, early designs.

Dials: 17th century dials are small and square, but later ones usually larger. **Break-arch dials** are normal from c. 1715, but many square dials continued to be made, especially for cottage clocks, which often had only one hand until almost the end of the 18th century. Painted dials were introduced c. 1775 but did not entirely supplant engraved brass.

Movements: 8-day and longer duration movements almost invariably rely on catgut, metal or nylon lines to support weights. 30 hour clocks usually have a single weight on an endless chain or rope.

Dial clock
English c.1850
Painted flat dial
Non-striking
Mahogany case

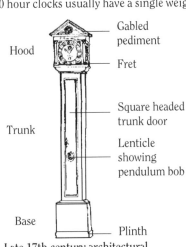

Hood

Gabled pediment

Fret

Square headed trunk door

Trunk

Lenticle showing pendulum bob

Base

Plinth

Late 17th century architectural longcase clock with square dial

Bracket or Mantel Clocks

In the 18th century, most examples will be English. In the 19th century French clocks are common while German and American copies of both occur in late 19th century.

Cases: English examples use the same woods as longcases, French ones often gilt metal or marble (sometimes slate). Some American clocks have cast iron cases.

Dials: English dials are smaller versions of longcase dials, normally without seconds; French dials are usually circular.

Movements: English, French and the best German examples are good quality, American ones less so.

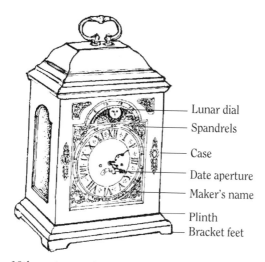

— Lunar dial
— Spandrels
— Case
— Date aperture
— Maker's name
— Plinth
— Bracket feet

18th century mahogany Bracket or Mantel clock
Arched ornamental dial showing phases of the moon, asymmetrical rococo spandrels, key escutcheon and matching blind escutcheon and corner pieces flanking the lunar dial.
Wavy minute hand.
Arabic minute figures, plain silvered chapter ring and large date aperture.
Maker's name at base of applied chapter ring.

MONUMENTS
Terms

Monuments inside churches range from large, elaborate canopied monuments to modest tablets affixed to the wall. The latter may simply carry inscriptions or they may include sculpture, carving and elaborate decoration. Costumed figures, lettering, symbols, heraldry and architectural features all appear on monuments and memorials. Many early monuments were coloured. Sadly, it is rare for any original colour to have survived, but later restorers have sometimes attempted to return medieval monuments to the rich hues in which they first appeared.

Monuments are full of clues to the history of the church and its community. They can tell us about the people who lived around the church and what they looked like, how wealthy the community was and why, why and how people died in different periods and many other details of their lives. They are also full of information on contemporary artistic style, philosophy and religious observance.

In the medieval period, all monuments stood on the floor, either against the wall or away from it. Wall monuments, entirely supported on the wall, were virtually unknown before the 16th century. Floor monuments were either large structures or simple floor slabs and generally lay over the mortal remains of the person or family they commemorate. Wall monuments, on the other hand, mostly consist of a tablet bearing an inscription in an architectural frame or cartouche, usually placed close to where the body had been interred.

Over time, monuments tend to have been moved around the church and may be nowhere near their original site.

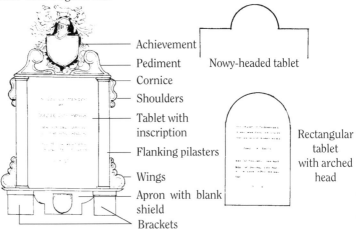

- Achievement
- Pediment — Nowy-headed tablet
- Cornice
- Shoulders
- Tablet with inscription
- Flanking pilasters — Rectangular tablet with arched head
- Wings
- Apron with blank shield
- Brackets

Inscriptions

AMDG	[ad majorem Dei Gloriam]	To the greater Glory of God
HIS	[hic iacet sepultus]	Here lies buried
HMP	[hoc monumentum posuit]	He erected this monument
INST	[in nomine Sanctae Trinitatis]	In the Name of the Holy Trinity
MS	[memoriae sacrum]	Sacred to the memory

MONUMENTS

Floor Slabs

Pre-1300 Slabs tapered from head to foot and were usually of local materials but Purbeck marble was commonly used for quality work. In the 12th century, slabs were ornamented with a variety of designs, carved in low relief or incised, often with a cross or symbol to indicate the profession of the deceased, but usually without lettering. Particularly after 1200, the slab might have borne a representation of the deceased in stone or later in brass but not a likeness. The same figure may be found in different churches.

13th-17th centuries Brasses, made of thin plates of copper/zinc alloy, were commonly set flush into the stone. Often only the indent of the brass survives today, the original having been lost or destroyed, but even a worn indent should give an idea of at least the shape of the brass. *Indents from which the brass is missing should be carefully described as they are of great interest.*

17th and 18th centuries Massive slabs of marble or bluish-grey stone were widely used, often with an achievement in bas-relief and an incised inscription in roman lettering.

19th century The making of figured brasses for monuments was revived as part of a general movement towards medieval revival but slabs of a wide variety of materials and styles are found.

12th century stone Coffin Lid with cross in relief

13th century slab with incised fleurée cross and fish and key symbols

14th century slab with indent of demi-figure, panel and two shields

17th century grey marble with bas-relief achievement in roundel above inscription

Tomb-chests

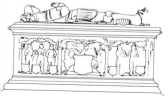

Tomb-chests are found with or without an effigy lying on top. They may be free-standing or recessed under a canopy against a wall. Free-standing tomb-chests may also be canopied in contemporary architectural styles.

Medieval tomb-chests may have blind arcading or be carved with weepers, angels or saints or with shields in quatrefoils, etc.

MONUMENTS

MONUMENTS
Effigies

Effigies

Before 1500, almost all effigies were recumbent. The earliest effigies had legs and hands in various positions, but after the mid-14th century legs were usually rigidly straight and hands placed together in prayer. Married couples may hold hands. Effigies were rarely portraits of the dead.

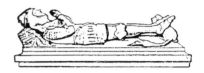

Figures carved on tomb-chests may help to date it. **Weepers** *(grieving members of the family, usually offspring)* occurred from the late 13th century (1); angels from the late 14th century (2); and saints in the 15th century (3).

1   2   3

The heads of effigies may be supported by pillows often held by angels. A knight's head may rest on a helmet, his feet against a couchant lion or other beast. Small figures of **bedesmen** (4) may be found on a couchant lion's back and pieces of armour may appear alongside the effigy.

4

Cadavers *(depictions of the deceased after death)* may occur alone or in addition to an effigy of the deceased in life and served as a memento mori.

1550 to early 17th century
Renaissance forms and decoration superseded Gothic, characterised by the use of columns, obelisks, strapwork, ribbonwork, grotesques, cherub-heads, allegorical figures etc. Effigy postures were stiff, recumbent, reclining or kneeling at prayer. Demi-figures appeared and, after 1600, sitting or standing figures. Roman lettering predominated, although Gothic was still used in the provinces. Effigies were dressed in contemporary costume. Painted and gilded alabaster was very popular. **Notable sculptors:** *Maximilian Colt, Gerard and Nicholas Johnson, William and Cornelius Cure.*

Early to mid-17th century
The classical style was now more refined, especially with the use of pediments on architectural canopies and frames; white and black marble competed with alabaster as popular materials. Effigies, mostly in contemporary dress, were found in a variety of poses and were generally less stiff with hands in various positions. Pedestal busts were introduced in this period. Sculptors' signatures were rare until the late 17th century. **Notable sculptors:** *Epiphanius Evesham, Nicholas Stone, Edward and Joshua Marshall, the Christmas family.*

c. 1660 to early 18th century
For the baroque tombs of this period, marble superseded alabaster. Recumbent and kneeling effigies were increasingly rare and relief medallion portraits appeared. Costume was usually contemporary but figures may wear Roman armour. Allegorical figures, particularly the Virtues, were common as were symbols of mortality and immortality. **Notable sculptors:** *Grinling Gibbons, John Nost, Thomas Green, Caius Gabriel Cibber, John Bushnell, Francis Bird, William and Edward Stanton.*

MONUMENTS

MONUMENTS
Floor and Wall Monuments

18th century

Architectural canopies disappeared after c.1750. Black or grey marble as a two-dimensional pyramid background to standing wall monuments and the combined use of different coloured marbles on one monument were popular. All previously mentioned effigy postures may be found but recumbent and kneeling were now rare. Figures were often dressed as Romans, sometimes in armour, sometimes loosely wrapped in toga-like garments, standing or reclining on a sarcophagus or against an urn. Small portrait medallions, busts, putti, urns, cartouches and symbols of mortality or immortality abounded. Much fine Rococo decoration is found. **Notable sculptors:** *Louis Francois Roubiliac, John Michael Rysbrack, Henry, Peter and Thomas Scheemakers, Henry Cheere, Joseph Wilton.*

Late 18th and early 19th centuries

A more restrained neo-classical style developed, inspired by ancient Greek models, especially the **stele** type of design (see p 215). Black and white marble were still popular, white increasingly so. Recumbent effigies began a gradual come-back, but very common in this period was a mourning female leaning over an urn or sarcophagus. Angels were frequently depicted, often receiving the deceased at death. Dress was stylised or contemporary, but naval and military effigies were often in uniform. **Notable sculptors:** *Joseph Nollekens, John Bacon and his son, John, Thomas Banks, Richard Westmacott, John Flaxman, Francis Chantrey, John Francis Moore.*

Victorian period

The Greek revival continued, but the Gothic style enjoyed a massive revival. Black and white marble were still common but alabaster was revived as a popular material. The use of canopies was revised, but particularly popular was the return of tomb-chests with recumbent effigies. Reclining, seated and standing effigies were much rarer. All styles of lettering were found and the monumental styles of other periods were sometimes employed. **Notable sculptors:** *Peter Hollins, Richard Westmacott the Younger, Joseph Boehm, Henry Armstead, Frederick Thrupp.*

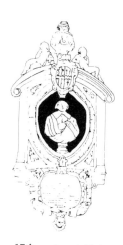

17th century tablet
Putto on either side of urn
Pedestal bust set in oval niche
Cartouche inscription tablet.

Late-18th century tablet
Closed urn
Panel carved in high relief,
curved and angular apron.

Cartouche with scrolls, flowers
and drapery, winged cherubs'
heads and an achievement.

**Mid-20th century rectangular brass
tablet**
with concave corners. Incised and
black inlaid cursive vine border.
Inscription, with flourished capitals,
beginning and ending with a
rubricated patée cross.

Stele
background

Early 19th century symbolism:
opium poppies *(the sleep of death)*; sickle
cutting rosebud *(death taking child)*

Lozenge tablet

Square tablet
with clipped,
chamfered or
canted corners
on ground of
conforming
shape.

MONUMENTS

MONUMENTS
Tomb-chest

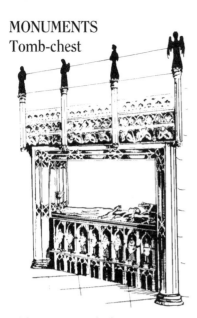

15th century tomb-chest

The tomb-chest of Alice, Duchess of Suffolk, d. 1475. Made of alabaster, it was probably erected soon after her death and stands between the Chancel and St John's Chapel.

The tomb-chest stands under a horizontal canopy of panelled stone, with an elaborate cornice of 3 tiers, the lowest formed of winged demi-figures of angels, each with hands folded on the breast; alternate angels have a crown or tonsure and one wears a fillet with a cross attached. Above the figures is a band of quatrefoils. The uppermost tier consists of elaborate quatrefoil cresting.

The canopy is divided vertically into 3 equal sections by stone shafts rising from foliated bosses and the capitals crowned with battlements on which stand carved wooden figures, 4 on each side *(figures should be described)*.

The tomb-chest consists of 2 tiers and the effigy. On top is the recumbent figure of the Duchess wearing widow's weeds over a contemporary dress with a ducal coronet on her head, a ring on the third finger of the right hand and the Garter on the left forearm. Her hands are closed in prayer and her head rests on a cushion supported by 2 angels on each side. Above her head is an elaborate canopy carved from a single block of alabaster. At her feet is a lion. Above her feet, on the panelling, is a bracket presumably for the image of a saint.

The side of the tomb-chest, on which the Duchess lies, is carved with a row of canopied niches occupied by frontally standing angels bearing shields with coats of arms. *(Angels should be described and arms blazoned).* Brass fillets on the cornice of the tomb-chest, on both north and south sides, carry the inscription in Black Letter in Latin.

Below the chest is an open space, enclosed by an arcade of 8 arches on either side, within which may be seen a cadaver clothed in a shroud. On the roof of this compartment, only to be seen by lying on the floor and looking through the arcades, are two paintings, St Mary Magdalene and St John on one side and the Annunciation on the other, a copy of which may be seen on the chancel side of the entrance to the Chapel.

17th century Memorial tablet

Rectangular architecturally framed alabaster tablet in memory of Richard Hampden d. 1662 and his wife Ann d.1663.

The cream alabaster tablet has a plain black marble border and an inscription incised in roman lettering, capitals and lower case. The marble frame is flanked by white veined, free-standing, angled Ionic columns which support a moulded cornice and segmental pediment with black tympanum, against which, and protruding above, is a carved and painted achievement. The motto is not displayed. *Arms should be blazoned.*

Grey marble, acanthus scrolled, tapering wing brackets flank the tablet against the wall.

The tablet and columns rest on a

black marble shelf supported by black and white erect consoles, between which, set against the wall, is a carved shield with painted coat of arms. *Arms should be blazoned.* Sculptor's signature N.O.N.E. on right edge of shelf.

18th century Memorial tablet

Sarcophagus with a putto sitting at either end of lid, one holding staff with cap of liberty, the other a scroll inscribed Magna Charta. In the centre of the lid is an acanthus spray with ribands stretching to the putti.

Directly above is an oval bas-relief with riband cresting and moulded frame, depicting an oak tree hung with coloured shields of Hampdens and allied families, rising from a scene of Chalgrove battlefield (where the parliamentarian, John Hampden, was mortally wounded in 1643).

On the front of the sarcophagus is an inscription in roman lettering, capitals and lower case, straight and slanting, relating to John Hampden d.1754 and his descent from John Hampden (above).

On the apron, between scrolled and acanthus decorated consoles and with an acanthus spray below the curved and angular lower edge, is the dedication in the same lettering. Only the shields are painted. *Arms should be blazoned.*

MONUMENTS
Wall Monument

18th century standing
wall monument

Large standing wall monument to Henry Petty, 1st Earl of Shelburne and his family in Roman dress.

The monument has a broad base with slightly projecting pedestal-like ends, bearing a large sarcophagus of grey marble, upon which reclines the effigy of the Earl in Roman tunic and toga, with the reclining figure of his wife holding an open book in her left hand. The front of the sarcophagus bears a portrait medallion of Sir William Petty, the Earl's father and founder of the family.

On each side of the monument there is a pair of composite unfluted columns supporting a broken triangular pediment, upon the apex of which is a garlanded urn. Upon one side reclines the figure of Justice and on the other, Truth. Below the feet of each is an urn. Under the arch of the pediment is an heraldic achievement carved in relief. *The arms should be blazoned.* Immediately below, against a tapering back panel swathed in drapery, are 2 putti among clouds holding a wreath over the head of the expiring nobleman.

Standing upon the pedestal on the dexter side stands the figure of the Earl's son James (died aged 40) dressed in Roman armour and robes. By his side sits his wife (died aged 32) with their son on her lap (died as an infant).

On the sinister side of the pedestal are two female figures in Roman dress and that of a young boy standing between them. These are the 2 daughters of the Earl, Julia and Anne, who died aged 23 and 30, and the Earl's son Charles who died aged 12.

The monument is made entirely of marble, the sarcophagus, columns, arch of variously coloured marble and the 12 life sized figures of white marble. There is a long inscription in the centre of the base incised in roman lettering, capitals and lower case. The monument is enclosed by iron railings erected in 1755.

MONUMENTS
Brasses

The fashion for brass rubbing has re-awakened interest in memorial brasses, many of which have survived in country churches in fine detail and represent an intriguing picture of the people they commemorate. Brasses were used for both secular and religious characters.

Most memorial brasses date from the 13th to 16th centuries, but there are some impressive 19th century ones, mostly ecclesiastical. The majority have figures as well as inscriptions; these are of great interest for accurate detail of costume, and should be fully described. Dress is of three kinds: civilian, military, ecclesiastical. Good reference books, such as Haines *(see FURTHER READING)*, will provide descriptions and vocabulary for contemporary costume, armour, and vestments. There may be several other elements set in one stone slab: inscriptions on plate, scrolls, or border fillet, groups of children, shields or badges. Some or all of these elements may be missing; in that case describe the shape and position of the indents from which they have gone. A rubbing taken of the brass can often be photographed more successfully than the brass itself.

Casement	slab into which a brass is set.
Indent or matrix	mark left in casement by missing brass.
Latten	alloy of copper and zinc with lead and tin used in the making of brasses.
Palimpsest	old brasses re-engraved on the reverse side.

15th century Memorial Brass
Memorial to Sir William Colwell, d 1443. Floor, centre of S aisle
Two figures are set beneath crocketed ogee arches of a double canopy with embattled entablature and pinnacled and buttressed shafting. Four shields of arms in a row between the arches and the entablature. *Arms should be blazoned.*

In a roundel within the man's canopy is a rebus device, a collet over a well. The roundel on the woman's side is blank. A Latin inscription in gothic lettering runs across the foot of the main panel, below this two groups of children, the girls on the left below their mother, the sons below the father. Surrounding all a border strip with roundels at the corners containing the emblems of the Evangelists; this has fragments of a marginal inscription, also in Latin in gothic letters, much of it now missing. Two prayer scrolls curving above the figures' heads contain inscriptions, in the same style of lettering.

The man, on the right, is bare-headed, with **bowl-crop** hair. He wears full plate armour including gauntlets and sabatons, sword and dagger. His feet, with rowel spurs, rest on a lion. His lady wears a heart-shaped headdress with short veil, a high-waisted **houppelande** with v-neck and long wide sleeves over an undergown with full sleeves gathered close at the wrist. A little dog nestles at her feet. The four daughters kneel, dressed like their mother. The four sons stand, and wear full-skirted gowns. All figures have their hands clasped in prayer.

Slab l.94cm x w.44cm; h. of main figures 40cm.

MONUMENTS

MONUMENTS
Brasses

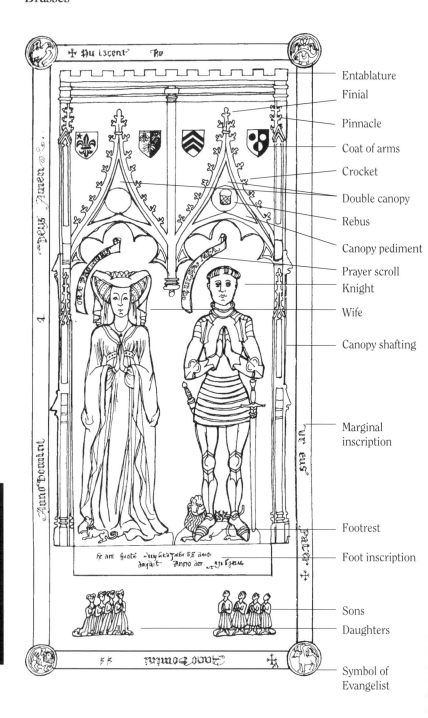

Entablature

Finial

Pinnacle

Coat of arms

Crocket

Double canopy

Rebus

Canopy pediment

Prayer scroll

Knight

Wife

Canopy shafting

Marginal
inscription

Footrest

Foot inscription

Sons

Daughters

Symbol of
Evangelist

Apart from keyboards and barrel organs, it is unusual to find working instruments in churches today. No working instrument should be handled without permission and supervision. Occasionally instruments used in 18th and 19th century church bands may survive. Always enquire about these.

Organs	see page 226
Chamber organs	free standing, small instruments described in the same way as organs.
Barrel organs	mechanical instruments which often resemble chamber organs. Pipes worked off large pinned barrels (like those of a musical box) turned by a handle. Name of maker, number of stops, number of barrels and list of tunes of each barrel are of interest Not all tunes may be hymns and sacred airs. Some barrel organs can also be played manually.
Carillons	bells struck from a form of keyboard and/or from pinned barrels. Located in church tower. Note the number of bells, name of bell founder and repertoire on any barrels.
Pianos	either winged, like a grand piano, or upright. Name of maker to be found on board above the keys. Note any special features like candle brackets or more than two pedals.

CHURCH BANDS

The instruments most commonly used to accompany church choirs in the 18th and 19th centuries were:

Flute, Flageolet, Clarinet or Oboe

simple tubes, probably in boxwood with a minimum of keys, usually for the little finger. Look for the name of the maker and serial number.

Serpent, Ophecleide, Bassoon or Bass Horn

low sounding instruments with long tubes, some curly (serpent) or folded (bassoon). Look for the name of the maker and serial number.

Key Bugle or Trombone

brass instruments, the bugle with padded keys; the trombone in two sections, one of which can be slid to and fro to lengthen or shorten the tubing and thus produce lower and higher sounding notes. The name of the maker may be stamped or engraved on the bell.

Violin, Cello or Double Bass

The name of the maker and other information may be on a label visible through the sound holes with a torch. In case these happen to be very early examples, take line drawings or photographs. Proportions of neck to fiddle and other details may indicate the date of the instrument. Note if the stringing is of gut or wire or both.

Pitchpipe

used to give the choir 'the note'.

INSTRUMENTS SEEN IN CARVING, STAINED GLASS AND PAINTINGS

No detail is too tiny to be noted in line drawings or photographs. The variety of early musical instruments is so bewildering that it is often difficult to identify one example accurately. Even then, different names are sometimes given to the same instrument. *Drawings and photographs should therefore make clear the following:*
How the instrument is held; number of strings on bowed and plucked instruments; precise position and shape of any sound holes; number of finger holes on wind instruments; their precise position and keys.

MUSICAL INSTRUMENTS
Stringed Instruments played with a bow

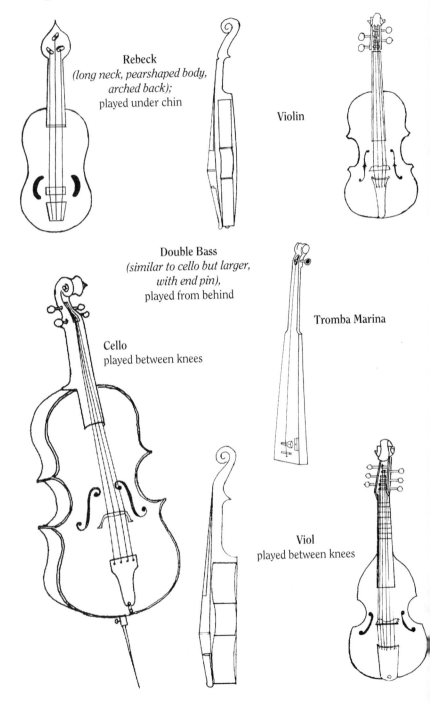

Rebeck
*(long neck, pearshaped body,
arched back);*
played under chin

Violin

Double Bass
*(similar to cello but larger,
with end pin),*
played from behind

Tromba Marina

Cello
played between knees

Viol
played between knees

MUSICAL INSTRUMENTS
Plucked Instruments

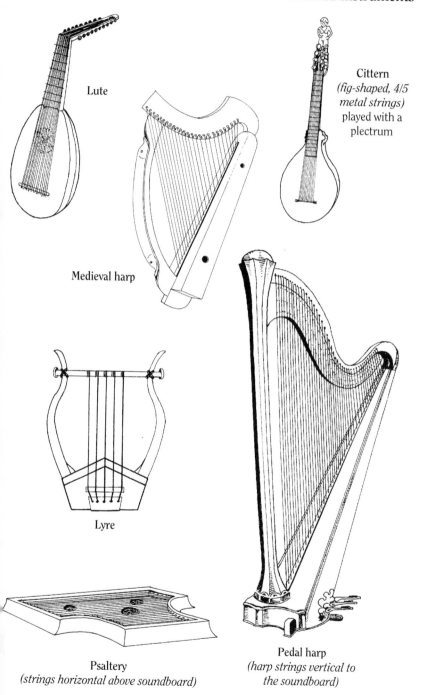

Lute

Cittern
(fig-shaped, 4/5 metal strings) played with a plectrum

Medieval harp

Lyre

Psaltery
(strings horizontal above soundboard)

Pedal harp
(harp strings vertical to the soundboard)

MUSICAL INSTRUMENTS
Wind Instruments

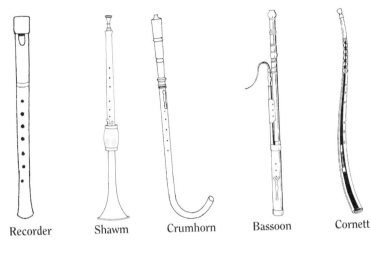

Recorder   Shawm   Crumhorn   Bassoon   Cornett

Buisine *(a medieval form of trumpet)*

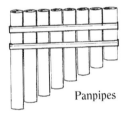

Panpipes

Natural trumpet

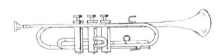

Trumpet

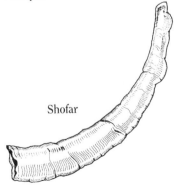

Shofar

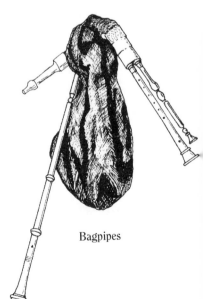

Bagpipes

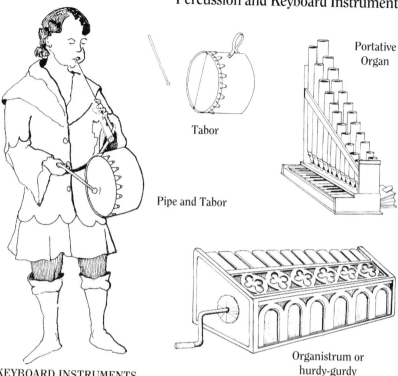

Tabor

Pipe and Tabor

Portative Organ

Organistrum or hurdy-gurdy

KEYBOARD INSTRUMENTS

Cottage Piano	small upright piano with iron frame introduced by Robert Wornum in 1813. Other makers include Southwell, William Allen, Stodart, Alphaeus Babcock, Conrad Mayer and Jonas Chickering.
Harmonium	small free reed keyboard instrument invented in 1840. Good examples made by the Paris firm of Alexandre, Pere & Fils.
Electronic Organ	instruments in which the sound is generated by often sophisticated electronic means which is amplified and played through loud speakers. These are either mounted within the instrument or more usually placed separately within the building. An early example of the type by Hammond was popular for a time but there are now very few of these left.
Pianola	automatic piano player driven by foot pedals played from perforated rolls, developed between 1887 - 1897.
Piano	either grand or upright. A trade label may give the name of the maker. Some best known makers are Erard, Broadwood, Bechstein, Steinway, Clementi.
Portative organ	small portable organs made from the 12th to mid 17th centuries. They were played by one person, who operated the bellows with the left hand and the keys with the right hand.
Positive organ	chamber organs designed for church or home use; a second person operated the bellows.

MUSICAL INSTRUMENTS
Organ

Since the middle ages, or even before, church music has been associated with the organ and perhaps a zenith of the art of organ building was reached in the late 17th and 18th centuries. None of these instruments survive in original form but the restoring zeal of the Victorians provided the majority of British churches with an organ which often is one of the dominant features of the building.

The most important 19th century organ builders were Hill, Willis, Gray & Davison and Walker but architects often had a hand in the design of cases to house them and examples by Pugin, Scott, Pearson and Bodley exist. A plate on the console will often reveal the name of the builder unless this has been replaced in later restoration work. It is harder to tell whether an organ is original to the building or has been removed from elsewhere.

It is rare that an organ of earlier date than 1840 survives, but occasionally parts have been incorporated into a later instrument. Early instruments usually have a note other than C as their lowest note.

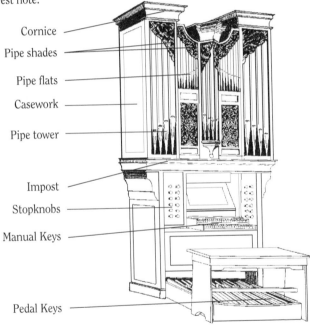

Cornice
Pipe shades
Pipe flats
Casework
Pipe tower
Impost
Stopknobs
Manual Keys
Pedal Keys

Case	the wood frame in which and behind which the pipes sit, which varies from a simple rack to a grand piece of furniture with a cornice and other embellishments.
Console	where the player sits with manual and pedal keyboards.
Flats	flat groups of pipes in the case.
Jambs	panels for the stops at the side of the keyboards which may be set at an angle.
Pipeshades	decorated features usually of carved wood, filling the gap between the sloping line of pipe tops and the frame of the case.

226

Stops or stopknobs	knobs which control pitch and tone mounted at the side on the jambs with ivory or plastic heads to indicate their function. Alternatively the stops may be in the form of ivory or plastic tabs set above the keyboards.
Towers	groups of pipes which often project forward at the sides and/or centre of the case, usually containing taller and fewer pipes than in the flats.

PIPES

Organ pipes are made of metal or wood, wood being common for the largest pipes. Metal pipes are often made of zinc but an alloy of tin and lead is better for tone. Where the tin content is high they may have a mottled appearance known as **spotted metal**. The front pipes are few in number and made for show so that they may be highly decorative, painted with diapered patterns. Most of the pipes will be out of sight inside the body of the case.

ACTION

Organs produce sound when wind is allowed to enter the pipes which stand vertically on and resonate against a rectangular chest or **soundboard** within the body of the organ. There are four types of action of which **mechanical** is the simplest form; indeed the musical value of this system has now been realised by most players and many new instruments use mechanical action.

Mechanical or Tracker Action	player directly controls the entry of wind into the pipes by a system of levers which open the valves called **pallets.**
Pneumatic Action	player's action conveyed by an air pressure system, identifiable by the presence of large amounts of small bore lead tubing inside the lower parts of the case; a popular system from 1880 to 1930.
Electro-Pneumatic Action	a modification of pneumatic action in which the primary energising of the entry of wind into the pipes is controlled by small electro-magnets.
Direct Electric Action	entry of wind into the pipes is controlled electrically by solenoids.

CONSOLE

The console will have at least one row of keys or manual and usually a row of pedal keys. Organs may have one to four manuals and even, very rarely, five. Each of the keyboards has a particular name and groups of stops relate to each.

Great Organ	the only manual or the lowest of two
Swell Organ	the upper of two or three manuals
Choir Organ	the lowest of three manuals
Solo Organ	the upper manual above the Swell in organs with more than three manuals
Pedal Organ	the sound is controlled by the pedal keys

Record details of materials and appearance; makers' name plate; any visible signs of repair; any evidence of maintenance (tuner's notebook); lowest and highest notes of each keyboard

WINDOWS
Terms

Since the introduction of stained glass in the 12th century the windows of a church have often been its chief glory. In the Middle Ages they were richly coloured storybooks. In spite of the iconoclasts, fine examples survive and re-assembled fragments are preserved in many churches. By the 16th century heraldic glass was important. In the 17th the religious climate condemned painted windows, much of what is to be found from that time is imported.

The 18th century designers used enamelling and treated windows as huge paintings. In the 19th century glaziers rediscovered the medieval tradition, and there was a splendid renaissance in stained and painted glass. With the vast increase in the number of churches in the second half of the century there was much stereotyped work, but the brilliant innovations of the Pre-Raphaelites, and those whom they inspired, gave an impetus which lasted into this century and which has produced its own idioms, including much abstract work.

Some glaziers signed their windows or included a glazier's mark (see p. 235). Others did not, but certain workshops can be recognised by their use of standard models such as angels, monograms and border motifs. Symbols and allegory play a large part, particularly with figures of saints or biblical scenes, and the iconography of pictorial windows is a fascinating study. *(See ATTRIBUTES & ALLEGORY p. 12-29 and FURTHER READING.)*

Texts and inscriptions are of two kinds: quotations, mostly scriptural; and commemorative or dedicatory inscriptions. The latter may be within the window or somewhere nearby.

The stonework frame of the window is usually in one of a series of well-defined Gothic styles, either original or reproduced, often with a number of minor lights in the upper tracery; these may also portray figures or small scenes related to the subject of the main lights. Windows without coloured glass usually consist of clear or tinted quarries *(small lozenge-shaped panes)*. They may however be leaded in complex geometric patterns, using glass of several pale shades.

Armatures	metal linking pieces of glass.
Blind tracery	areas with blank stone or other infill, not glass.
Calm	see leading.
Canopy	framework either architectural (arches, turrets, pillars, etc.) or foliate around the figures contained in the lights.
Cusp	projecting point between foils.
Dedication	commemoration message for donor or event.
Enamelling	*See METAL: Terms (p.101).*
Eyelets	smallest elements in tracery.
Fillets	narrow glass borders next to stonework frame, plain or beaded.
Foil	concave element in stonework, between cusps; heads of arches are often trefoil or cinquefoil, tracery lights may be of any number of foils.

Grisaille — monochromatic patterns on clear glass in yellow, grey, or brown, used from 13th century and copied in 19th and 20th centuries (see **Stamped quarries**).

Hachures — small shading lines.

Heraldic — containing coats of arms.

Inscription — **Memorial**: to persons, family or group or **Commemorative**: of event or institution.

Leading — framing of individual pieces of glass with lead calms of H-section, usually outlining each area of one colour.

Lights — sections of window divided by transoms or mullions.

Lined out — outlined in black paint or enamel.

Quarries — small regular diamond-shaped panes; any with horizontal and vertical leading are called **square quarries**.

Stained glass — common term for coloured glass; shading is added by painting and other techniques. (see **Silver stain**).

Silver stain — the only glass which is truly stained, by either silver sulphide or chloride, to produce various shades of yellow glass; process discovered in the early 14th century.

Stamped quarries — 19th century process for mass production of quarries decorated with a monochrome motif.

Tracery — ornamental shapes formed by the branching of mullions in the upper part of a window.

Texts — quotations from Bible or other sources

Tracery lights — sections of the ornamental tracery formed by the branching of mullions in the upper part of a window.

WINDOWS

Oriel
when
supported on
corbels

Lucarne on a
spire
Dormer
on a house roof

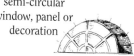

Lunette
semi-circular
window, panel or
decoration

Wheel Window
round window with
radiating tracery

Rose Window
round window with concentric tracery

*Note the sequence in which round window
lights should be numbered*

WINDOWS
Types

Saxon and Norman (Romanesque) windows were small and usually unglazed. This was for security and because of limited building knowledge. Builders did not dare to weaken the wall with large openings. English glass-making largely died out after the departure of the Romans and imports from France and Germany were costly. During the Middle Ages building confidence grew, times were less troubled, windows became larger. Arch heads followed the Gothic pattern (see p.7). Tracery designs are illustrated on p. 231-2.

With the return of classicism the Renaissance windows were round-headed, for example, Sir Christopher Wren's 17th century churches. He also used the circular **oeil de boeuf** form as did Baroque architects of the early 18th century. With the 19th century Gothic Revival, the pointed arch and coloured glass were once more designed, a pattern which continued well into the 20th century.

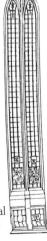

Norman
(Romanesque)
window

Saxon window openings

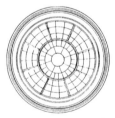

Wren oeil de boeuf
(bull's eye) window
1670-80

Wren window, 1685

Rose window,
Pearson, 1875

Baroque oeil de boeuf window, 1712

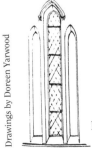

Lancet window,
1845

Maufe Cathedral
window, 1939

WINDOWS

Tracery is the term used to describe the varied forms of stone and glass decoration of the window head during the Middle Ages. The earliest window lights (see p. 230) which evolved after the Gothic introduction of the pointed arch (see p. 7) were single lancets. These were narrow, undecorated lights. Soon it became customary to group the lancets (3, 5 or 7) under one arch moulding. The next stage was to create a single window under the encompassing arch which would be divided vertically by mullions. The solid stone head was pierced by cut out shapes: this was **plate tracery**. From this derived **bar tracery** where the glass area became greater and the stonework narrower. Windows grew steadily larger and were divided by a greater number of vertical mullions and horizontal transoms. Designs of the head developed from reticulated (**net**) forms, to geometrical, curvilinear (**flowing lines**) and finally to the panel (**perpendicular**) types. Each part of the design was shaped in small arcs of stone called **foils**. The number of foils were indicated by the prefix: trefoil (3); quatrefoil (4); cinquefoil (5) or multifoil (many). The points of the foils are called **cusps**. Circular windows were common. These were decoratively traceried. The early types were plate tracery wheel windows; these had radiating spokes. Later came the rose window with geometric or curvilinear tracery.

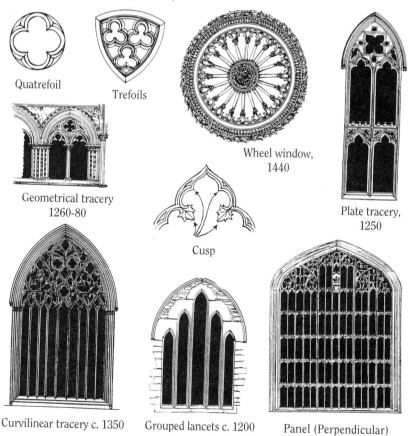

Quatrefoil

Trefoils

Wheel window,
1440

Geometrical tracery
1260-80

Cusp

Plate tracery,
1250

Curvilinear tracery c. 1350

Grouped lancets c. 1200

Panel (Perpendicular)
tracery, 1485-1509

WINDOWS
Tracery

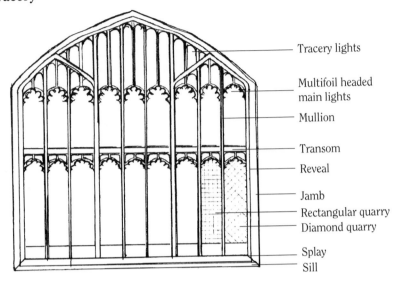

- Tracery lights
- Multifoil headed main lights
- Mullion
- Transom
- Reveal
- Jamb
- Rectangular quarry
- Diamond quarry
- Splay
- Sill

Window of 9 multifoiled lights, arranged in triplets in two stages with tracery of 15th century rectilinear form.

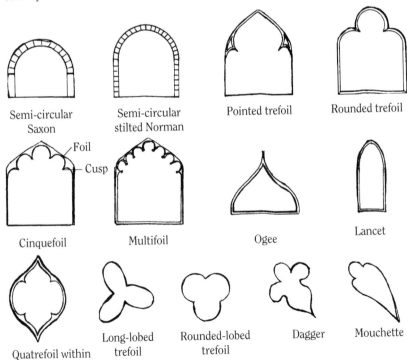

Semi-circular Saxon	Semi-circular stilted Norman	Pointed trefoil	Rounded trefoil

Foil
Cusp

Cinquefoil	Multifoil	Ogee	Lancet

Quatrefoil within an ogival	Long-lobed trefoil	Rounded-lobed trefoil	Dagger	Mouchette

232

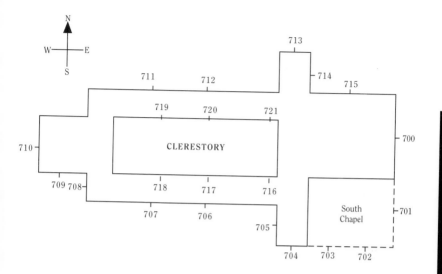

Number the windows clockwise from the E window (700) all round the ground floor, including porches and vestries. Then clockwise again round any clerestory, and finally the upper stories of the tower. Number a plan of the church to show positions of all windows. (Sections of the church, such as chapels, should be labelled with the names used by the congregation).

Aim to have a photograph of each window, or type of window. Windows with tracery lights should have a diagram on the same page as their description, with the lights numbered from left to right and top to bottom. Sections of the descripion are then identified by these numbers, shown in brackets. (To avoid confusion with the format Nos. 1 to 10).

Follow the arrangements shown in Sample Pages and p. 234. Having described the stonework in general terms, proceed to describe shape and contents of tracery lights. For pictorial windows, preface the description of the individual main lights with the name of the subject (if spread over all lights), and describe any elements common to all lights, (e.g. background, borders, angels, scrolls).

Give the words of bible quotations, etc, as you come to them in the description. If the source is given, make it clear whether that was in the window or is your research. Commemorative inscriptions have their text quoted at 9. Do not forget to record any identifying glaziers' marks, signatures, etc, preferably accompanied by sketch or photograph.

Close-up colour photographs of important elements of a window greatly enhance the Record, and may replace some of the descriptive text otherwise necessary. Remember to quote all references and sources.

WINDOWS
Late 19th Century Window

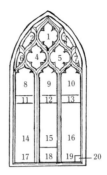

Stonework: Late 19th century, 3 trefoil headed lights and 7 traceries in 14th century Reticulated style.

Tracery Lights

1.	Dove descending amidst 3 stars in purple night sky.
2&3.	Sprig of oak leaves with acorn in natural colouring against a light yellow ground.
4.	Crescent moon against dark blue sky.
5.	Sun against light blue sky.
6&7	A trefoil lined out in black against a pale yellow ground.
Main Lights:	Adoration of the Shepherds and the Magi.
8,9&10	In each a group of 3 angels with multicoloured wings and wearing white girdled tunics. Each central angel playing a musical instrument, rebeck, harp and tabor respectively, outer ones all singing.
11,12,&13	Text in Gothic capitals and lower case, painted in black on a pale yellow ground. It is difficult to decipher but enough to identify with Matt.2:2 *We have seen his star/in the East and are come/to adore him.*
14.	3 shepherds, placed vertically, upper two standing, one kneeling, all wear nomads' head-dresses, each in a different brightly coloured cloak, red, yellow and blue; two hold crooks, the kneeling shepherd does not appear to have one.
15.	Virgin Mary seated with infant Christ on her knee, Joseph standing behind. Virgin wears a royal blue mantel with gold trimming. Infant Christ swaddled. Joseph wears a dark red cloak over a long green tunic. The Virgin and Joseph each have a yellow nimbus, the Christ child has a yellow and white cruciform nimbus.
16.	3 Magi similarly placed to the shepherds: Caspar in purple robe with fur cape-collar attached with a tied cord; Melchior in rich brown robe; Balthazar, the youngest kneeling and bearing a gift, wears a white tunic and emerald green super-tunic, with his crown on the ground in front of him.
	Plain white dado behind all 3 scenes, band of light blue sky above.
17&19	A kneeling angel dressed in a white robe, with flame coloured wings and nimbus, yellow stain seaweed background.
18.	Old Testament Altar of Sacrifice in natural colours against a green ground.
20.	Artist's signature. Mark of a daisy within a bell: Margaret Bell.

Reginald Bell

Clayton & Bell

Clayton & Bell

John Clement
Bell

Alfred Bell

M C Farrar
Bell

William Wailes

C C Townshend
& J Howson

Goddard
& Gibbs

Rachel de
Montmorency

Hugh
Easton

Horace
Wilkinson

J W Kubler

E F
Brickdale

Edward
Jenkins
Prest

WINDOWS
Makers' Marks

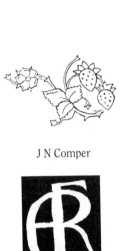

J N Comper

Pope & Parr

H W Bryans

Martin Travers

A R Fisher

T Willement

J N Lawson

J E Nuttgens

Chapel Studios

Caroline
Benyon

Percy Bacon & Bros.

Lawrence
S Lee

J Wippell & Co
Exeter
pre - 1970 & 1980 - present

Wippell Mowbray
Church Furnishing Ltd
1970 - 1980

Ray
Bradley

Henry James
Salisbury

N H J Westlake

Tom Carter Shapland

H J Stammers

A C W Younger

Robert Hendra and
Geoffrey Harper

Moira Forsyth

K Parsons Paul Woodroffe H W Harvey

Martin Webb

Powell & Sons of Whitefriars

Christopher
Webb

Geoffrey Webb

C.E. Kempe
pre 1907

C.E. Kempe & Co Ltd
1907-1934

Francis
Skeat

Francis
Skeat

W. Holland
Warwick

William
Warrington

M.E. Aldrich
Rope

J.C.
Bewsey

FURTHER READING

Inside Churches can be no more than an introduction to the decoration and furnishings encountered in British churches. In each subject area there are many helpful secondary sources, some of which are recommended here. Some interesting primary sources may also be available through the incumbent of the parish or through county record offices.

Recognised Church Recorders may also refer queries to various professionals through the National Association of Decorative and Fine Arts Societies.

General Reading

Addleshaw, G W O and Etchells, Frederick	The Architectural Setting of Anglican Worship *Faber and Faber, 1948*
Anson, Peter	Fashions in Church Furnishings, 1840-1940 *Faith Press, 1960*
Betjeman, Sir John	Collins Guide to Parish Churches of England and Wales *Collins, 1980*
Cox, Charles and Harvey, Alfred	English Church Furniture *E P Publishing, 1973*
Howkins, Christopher	Discovering Church Furniture *Shire Publications, 1980*
Lewis, Philippa and Darley, Gillian	Dictionary of Ornament *Macmillan, 1986*
Miller, Judith (ed.)	Miller's Pocket Antiques Fact File *Mitchell Beazley, 1988*
Pevsner, Sir Nikolaus and others	The Buildings of England *Penguin*
Randall, Gerald	Church Furnishing and Decoration in England and Wales *Batsford, 1980*
Royal Commission on Historical Monuments, England	Inventories of historical monuments *HMSO*
Stafford, Maureen and Ware, Dora	An Illustrated Dictionary of Ornament *Allen and Unwin, 1974*
	The Victoria History of the Counties of England *Oxford University Press*
Victoria and Albert Museum catalogue	Victorian Church Art *(November 1971-January 1972)*

Architecture

Child, Mark	Discovering Church Architecture *Shire Publications, 1976*
Council for British Archaeology	Recording a Church: an illustrated glossary *1984*
Curl, James Stevens	English architecture: an illustrated glossary *David and Charles, 1986*
Fletcher, Sir Bannister	History of Architecture *Athlone Press, 1975*

Harries, J	Discovering Churches
	Shire Publications, 1972
Harris, John and Lever, Jill	Illustrated Glossary of Architecture 850-1830
	Faber and Faber, 1966, 1992
Yarwood, Doreen	Encyclopaedia of Architecture
	Batsford

Attributes & Allegory

Child, Heather and Colles, Dorothy	Christian Symbols, Ancient and Modern
	Bell and Hyman, 1971
Farmer, David Hugh	The Oxford Dictionary of Saints
	Oxford University Press, 1978
Ellwood Post, W	Saints, Signs and Symbols
	SPCK, 1964
Hall, James	Dictionary of Subjects and Symbols in Art
	John Murray, 1987
Hume, Edward	Symbolism in Christian Art

Costume

Borg, A	Arms and Armour in Britain
	HMSO, 1977
Blair, C	European and American Arms c. 1100-1850
	Batsford, 1962
Mayo, Janet	The History of Ecclesiastical Dress
	Batsford 1985
Cunnington, P	A Dictionary of English Costume
	A and C Black 1960
Cunnington, P	Handbook of English Costume (various volumes)
	Faber and Faber 1973
Yarwood, Doreen	English Costume from the 2nd Century BC to 1960
	Batsford

Decoration

Brackett, O	English Furniture Illustrated
	Hamlyn
Croft-Murray, Edward	Decorative Mural Painting in England, 1537 - 1837
	Country Life, 1962
Croft-Murray, Edward	Decorative Painting in England, the 18th and 19th centuries
	Country Life, 1970
Gloag, J	A Short Dictionary of Furniture
	Allen and Unwin, 1952
Meyer, F S	Handbook of Ornament
	Dover, 1957
Rouse, Clive	Medieval Wall Paintings
	Shire Publications, 1991
Ware, D and Stafford, M	An Illustrated Dictionary of Ornament
	Allen and Unwin, 1974

Heraldry

Brooke-Little, J P (ed)	Boutell's Heraldry *F Warne 1978*
Burke, Sir John Bernard	The General Armory of England, Scotland, Ireland and Wales *Tabard, 1966*
Frear, Jacqueline	Discovering Heraldry *Shire Publications*
Fox-Davies, A C	A Complete Guide to Heraldry *Nelson, 1969*
Friar, Stephen	A New Dictionary of Heraldry *Alpha Books*
MacKinnon, Charles	The Observer Book of Heraldry *Warne*
Moncrieffe, Sir Iain and Pottinger, Don	Simple Heraldry Cheerfully Illustrated *Nelson, 1952*
Papworth, John Wood	Papworth's Ordinary of British Armorials *Tabard, 1961*
Summers, Peter	Hatchments in Britain (various volumes) *Phillimore, 1974-1980*

Lettering

Johnston, E	Writing and Illuminating and Lettering *Pitman, 1906*
Macklin, H W	The Brasses of England *E P Group. 1975*

Ceramics

Barnard, Julian	Victorian Ceramic Tiles *Studio Vista, 1972*
Cushion, J P and Honey, W B	A Handbook of Pottery and Porcelain Marks *Faber and Faber*
Eames, Elizabeth S	English Medieval Tiles *British Museum, 1985*
Eames, Elizabeth S	Medieval Craftsmen: English Tilers *British Museum, 1992*
Hughes, G Bernard	The Country Life Collectors' Pocket Book

Metal

Bambery, Angela	Old Sheffield Plate *Shire Publications, 1988*
Banister, Judith	English Silver Hallmarks *Foulsham, 1970*
Camp, John	Discovering Bells and Bellringing *Shire Publications, 1975*
Cotterell, Howard Herschel	Old Pewter, its makers and marks *C E Tuttle, 1963*
Hollister-Short, G J	Discovering Wrought Iron *Shire Publications, 1970*

Hull, Charles	Pewter
	Shire Publications, 1992
Oman, Charles	English Church Plate
	Oxford University Press, 1957
Peal, Christopher	British Pewter and Britannia Metal
	John Gifford, 1971
Walters, H B	Church Bells of England
	Oxford University Press, 1977

Paper

Briquet, Charles M	Les Filigranes
	Paris, 1907
Darley, L S	Introduction to Book Binding
	Faber and Faber, 1965
Heawood, Edward	Watermarks etc
	1950
Tate, W E	The Parish Chest: A Study of the Records of Parochial Administration in England
	Cambridge University Press, 1969

Stone

Kilburn, Father E	A Walk around the Church of the London Oratory
	Sand and Co, 1966

Textiles

Kelly, Francis and Schwabe, Randolph	A Short History of Costume and Armour, 1066-1800
	David and Charles, 1972
Dean, Beryl	Ecclesiastical Embroidery
	Batsford, 1958
Fokker, Nicolas	Persian and Other Oriental Carpets for Today
	Allen and Unwin, 1973
Hands, M H	Church Needlework
	Faith Press, 1957

Wood

Chinnery, V	Oak Furniture: The British Tradition
	Antique Collectors Club, 1988
Corkhill, Thomas	A Glossary of Wood
	Stobart and Sons, 1984
Edwards, R	A Shorter Dictionary of English Furniture
	Hamlyn, 1964
Gloag, J	A Short Dictionary of Furniture
	Allen and Unwin, 1952
Hayward, C H	English Period Furniture
	Evans, 1971
Howard, F E & Crossley, F H	English Church Woodwork
	Batsford 1927
Jervis, Simon	The Woodwork of Winchester Cathedral
	Friends of Winchester Cathedral, 1976

241

Joy, E T	The Country Life Book of Chairs
	Hamlyn, 1967
Smith, J C D	A Guide to Church Woodcarving: misericords and bench-ends
	David and Charles, 1974
Smith, J C D	Church Woodcarvings: A West Country Study
	David and Charles, 1969
Tracy, Charles	English Medieval Furniture and Woodwork
	Victoria & Albert Museum, 1990

Clocks

Baillie, G H	Watchmakers and Clockmakers of the World
	NAG Press, 1976 Vol I
Beeson, C F C	English Church Clocks, 1280-1850
	Phillimore, 1971
Betts, J	The National Trust Pocket Guide to Clocks
	Octopus, 1985
Loomes, B	Watchmakers and Clockmakers of the World
	NAG Press, 1976 Vol II
Rose, R E	English Dial Clocks
	Antique Collectors Club, 1978
Smith, A	Clocks and Watches
	1975

Memorials & Monuments

Chapman, Leigh	Brasses and Brass Rubbing
	Shire Publications, 1987
Esdaile, Kathleen	English Church Monuments 1510 - 1840
	Batsford 1946
Greenhill, Frank	Incised Effigal Slabs
	Faber and Faber, 1976
Kemp, Brian	English Church Monuments
	Batsford, 1980
Kemp, Brian	Church Monuments
	Shire Publications, 1988
Macklin, H W	The Brasses of England
	EP Group 1975
Mill Stephenson, B A	A List of Monumental Brasses in the British Isles
	Headley, 1926
Norris, Malcolm	Monumental Brasses: the Craft
	Faber and Faber, 1978
Norris, Malcolm	Monumental Brasses: the Memorials
	Phillips and Page, 1989
Stone, Lawrence	Sculpture in Britain: the Middle Ages
	Penguin, 1955
Tummers H A	Early Secular Effigies in England: the Thirteenth Century
	Brill, 1980
Whinney, Margaret	Sculpture in Britain: 1530-1830
	Penguin, 1964

Musical Instruments

Baker, David	The Organ
	Shire Publication, 1991
Clutton, C and Niland, A	The British Organ
	Batsford, 1963
Hindley, G	Musical Instruments
	Hamlyn, 1971
Remnant, Mary	Musical Instruments - an illustrated History.
	Batsford, 1989

Windows

Hall, James	Dictionary of Subjects and Symbols in Art
	Murray, 1989
Harrison, K	An Illustrated Guide to the Windows of King's College Chapel, Cambridge
Harrison, Martin	Victorian Stained Glass
	Barrie and Jenkins, 1980
Harries, John	Discovering Stained Glass
	Shire Publications, 1980
Kirby, H T	The Stained Glass Artist
	British Society of Master Glass Painters' Journal Vol X, No 4 , 1950-51
Lee, Lawrence, Seddon, George and Stephens, Francis	Stained Glass
	Mitchell Beazley, 1976
Sewter, A Charles	The Stained Glass of William Morris and his Circle
	Yale University Press, 1974-5

INDEX